D1346412

ST MARY REDCLIFFE: AN ARCHITECTURAL HISTORY

ST MARY REDCLIFFE
An architectural history

MICHAEL QUINTON SMITH

redcliffe

First published in 1995
by Redcliffe Press Ltd., Bristol
in an edition of 1,250 copies,
of which 125 were numbered
and signed by the author.

ISBN 1 872971 58 X

The publication of this book has been assisted by the Publications
Committee, the Arts Faculty Research Fund, and the History of
Art Department of the University of Bristol.

British Library Cataloguing in Publication Data
A catalogue record for this book is available
from the British Library.

Typeset by Westcountry Books and printed by
Longdunn Press Ltd., Bristol

CONTENTS

Frontispiece: *Stained glass*: Madonna and child, *fifteenth century, reset in west window of the tower*. Photo: *Gordon Kelsey*.

For Rebecca and Tobias,
both born in Bristol

LIST OF ILLUSTRATIONS

Frontispiece: *Stained glass, Madonna and Child*

ACKNOWLEDGEMENTS

At a most crucial stage in the preparation of this material, when finishing was proving harder than starting, the Publications Committee of Bristol University gave me financial support and encouragement. Further help towards the cost of publication was given by the Arts Faculty Research Fund and the History of Art Department. My colleagues in History of Art rearranged things so that I could have study leave during which I made final revisions to the text.

I must thank a host of students who have patiently listened to my latest ideas on The Redcliffe Problem. Many friends and colleagues have helped me, especially Joe Bettey, the late Basil Cottle, Nora Hardwick, David Kinmont, the late Bryan Little, Anthea Paice, Elizabeth Ralph, Geoffrey Robinson, the late James Sherborne, and Sheena Stoddard. Roxanne Besse, Simon Bristow, Damian Gillie, Gordon Kelsey, Tobias Smith and the late Reece Winstone all helped me with photography. I thank Tony Whatmough, vicar of St. Mary Redcliffe for his help and encouragement.

The former vicar, Canon David Frayne, and his staff and all the official and unofficial helpers in the church have all been most obliging, suffering my puzzling and questioning, often in the company of groups of students.

None but myself is responsible for my mistakes and misinterpretations:

> No more, dear Smith, the hackneyed tale renew:
> I own their censure, I approve it too.
> ...
> What I think right I ever will pursue,
> And leave you liberty to do so too.

> Thomas Chatterton: *The Defence*.

INTRODUCTION

Yet in the church I had rather speak five words with my understanding, that by my voice I might teach others also, than ten thousand words in an unknown tongue.

1 Corinthians XIV. 19

This book is a brief history of the architecture of St. Mary Redcliffe rather than yet another guidebook. My main aim has been to explain why the church looks the way it does. It took about four hundred years to build and rebuild, but almost as significant are the four hundred and fifty years since the Reformation, during which time the church has been transformed in ways closely related to the changes in the character of the Church of England.

St. Mary Redcliffe has inspired a rich literature, and to help anyone who wishes to explore further, suggestions for further reading are included either in the text or at the end of each chapter and summarised in a select bibliography.

Various spellings acknowledge the topographical situation of the church, including Radeclyve, Radcleve, Radeclivia, Redcliff and Redcliffe. The last two forms are both still current: for consistency one spelling has been adopted throughout this book, except in quotations.

In the course of revising earlier versions I have with reluctance omitted much that is interesting: but it is hoped that a shorter book, arranged chronologically, has advantages over a more cautious and much longer chronicle. In the disentangling of fact from fiction, accepted in varying degrees by many subsequent writers, any author needs to tread with great wariness. One of the pleasures in preparing this book has been reading so much contradictory and contentious material.

I hope that friends and colleagues, especially fellow-contributors to the publications of the Bristol Branch of the Historical Association, will regard it as a compliment that I have relied so heavily on their specialist researches, and pray that I shall be forgiven when I have ventured to abbreviate, simplify or even dispute their conclusions. Many of my ideas were stimulated by conversations in and around the University.

But the greatest pleasure has been spending quiet hours in the church itself.

Ultra Avonam. Redcliffe longe pulcherr.
omnium ecclesa.

So noted John Leland in about 1550, expressing an opinion which admits no dispute.

1

SITE AND ARCHAEOLOGY

*Having laid out the alleys and determined the streets,
we have next to treat of the choice of building sites
for the temples ... Jupiter, Juno and Minerva should
be on the highest point. Mercury in the forum,
Apollo and Bacchus near the theatre, Hercules at the
circus, Mars outside the city, and Venus at the
harbour.*

Vitruvius

Until well into the twentieth century the first great building of Bristol to be seen by visitors approaching from London or the south would have been St. Mary Redcliffe. It would have been an unforgettable landmark, above the masts of the shipping which lay along the quaysides even into the very centre of the city.

Nowadays, though that peculiarly Bristol experience has been destroyed forever, the ancient and once quite distinct settlement on the Red Cliff, across the river from Bristol, remains a separate part of the huge, sprawling modern city.

As any visitor to the church today soon discovers, the members of the congregation of St. Mary Redcliffe still think of themselves as a select community which is separate, distinct and undoubtedly superior to the rest of Bristol.

In part this is due to historical factors. Novices should be warned that several writers place Redcliffe in the wrong county, which can be a nuisance when searching through lists or an index. Throughout the early middle ages, Redcliffe was in Somerset - certainly never in Gloucestershire. Similarly, it needs to be remembered that the parish was in the diocese of Bath and Wells while Bristol was within the diocese of Worcester. Not till 1540 was St. Mary Redcliffe included in the newly-created diocese of Bristol , where it has remained apart from the short period 1836-1845 when it was transferred back to Bath and Wells.

The geographical context also deserves some attention before we proceed to the strictly architectural history of the church. The earliest settlements in the area would, it can be presumed, have been on the drier ground above the marshy banks of the river. This historic geographical siting of St. Mary Redcliffe on a hill to the south of the Avon, and quite independent of the settlements which in the end formed Bristol, is shown vividly in the earliest printed maps and views, one of the most attractive of them being James Millerd's perspective 'An Exact Delineation of the Famous City of Bristol and suburbs thereof...' first published in 1673.

As yet no evidence has been discovered to support the legend, retold by William Barrett in 1789, that a church had been founded on the Redcliffe as early as 789 by a Saxon king named Brightvicos or Brithwick. Indeed the existence of any such king is probably fictional, and is presumably based on an idea promoted by Thomas Chatterton, who in *A Discourse on Brigstowe* went so far as to provide a quite abominably inept drawing of what Brightvicos' church looked like. If

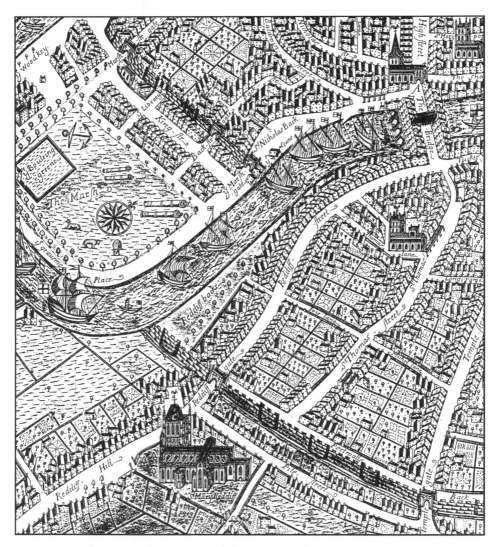

The site of St. Mary Redcliffe, across the river and outside the city walls. Detail from Millerd's Plan of Bristol, 1673. City Art Gallery, Bristol.

there was so early a church the present building would, taking into account all the rebuildings and restorations, be the fifth on the site. But as the recent excavations of St. Augustine the Less on the other side of the river have shown, even a late medieval church may be on a site occupied - to the archaeologist's surprise - from a date much earlier than any reliable documentary evidence.

The early parochial history of the area in which St. Mary Redcliffe stands is still far from clear. In the entries for Somerset in Domesday Book, 1086, is found the record of Bedminster, the area south of the River Avon and including Redcliffe: it contained three slaves, 25 villagers and 22 smallholders, a mill and a priest - and thus, by implication, a church also. The name Bedminster has indeed by some authors been interpreted as Bede-Minster, that is to say 'church of the monastery'.

W.H. Bartlett's romantic view of the church from the water.
Engraving c.1830. City Art Gallery.

Henry I, in the period 1107-1125, granted the church of Bedminster to Old Sarum (Salisbury) cathedral and it is thus that the first mention of the church of St. Mary Redcliffe occurs in the Register of Saint Osmund where a charter of Henry II, dating from c. 1160, confirms the bestowal of the churches of Bedminster, Leigh (i.e. Abbot's Leigh, beyond Clifton Gorge) and Redcliffe on the cathedral. From later entries in this Sarum Register we can derive the names of some of the earliest vicars of the church.

It is still possible to sense how dramatic the site of the original church must have been. The church stands on the edge of a cliff, with Redcliffe Hill sloping away to the south. Northwards, towards the centre of Bristol and below the cliff it must, as the early charters suggest, have been wet: '... men dwelling in the marsh near the bridge at Bristow...' The ground level was clearly several feet lower than it is now, as has been proved by the archaeologists who have in recent years excavated at various points along the river's edge, especially on the site of Canynges' House at 95-97 Redcliffe Street. In the thirteenth century the wharf was very much closer to the church than it is now - at about the line of the exit westwards to the bridge from the roundabout on Redcliffe Way. Northwards, the Portwall - the outer wall of Bristol built in the thirteenth century - was pierced by Redcliffe Gate. This stood roughly where Redcliffe Street now meets the same busy roundabout.

It is recorded in the *Gesta Stephani*, 1138, that 'Bristol is almost the richest city of all the country, receiving merchandise by sailing ships from lands near and far.' By the end of the century, the many churches, some of which (All Saints, St. Mary-le-Port, St. Peter, Christchurch, St. John, St. Stephen, St. Nicholas, St. James, St. Thomas, St. Philip and Jacob) still survive - witnessed the piety and prosperity of Bristol. But none of them was ever so splendid as St. Mary Redcliffe. It has always held the pre-eminence among the parish churches of Bristol which it retains to this day.

FURTHER READING

David Walker: *Bristol in the Early Middle Ages*. (Bristol Branch of the Historical Association, 1971)

James Sherborne: *The Port of Bristol in the Middle Ages*. (Bristol Branch of the Historical Association, 1965)

M.Q. Smith: *The Medieval Churches of Bristol*. (Bristol Branch of the Historical Association, 1970)

Chatterton's drawing of a supposed pre-conquest church is reproduced in D.S. Taylor: *The Complete Works of Thomas Chatterton* (1971), vol. I, p.94 and pl.1.

For connections with Salisbury, Edith Williams: 'The Prebend of Bedminster with Redcliffe in Salisbury Cathedral', in C. Powell: *St. Mary Redcliffe and its Restoration* (1933), pp. 24-26.

For early documents see:

C. & T. Thorn (eds.): *Domesday Book: 8: Somerset* (1980)

Register of St. Osmund, Rolls Series 78 (1898), especially vol. I, pp. 203 and 270; vol. II, pp. 73, 81-83.

F.B. Bickley (ed.) *The Little Red Book of Bristol*, vol. I (1900), pp. 22-23.

N.D. Harding (ed.): *Bristol Charters 1155-1373* (Bristol Record Soc. I, 1930), pp. 4-5, 18-19 and 22-23.

For an historical account of the whole area, L.G.W. Vear: *South of the Avon: Glimpses of Old Bedminster Life* (1978)

M. Manson: *Bristol Beyond the Bridge* (1988)

For recent discoveries, see

B. Williams: *Excavations in the Medieval Suburb of Redcliffe, Bristol* (City of Bristol Museum and Art Gallery, 1981). This includes a short history of the suburb.

J. Shackleton & J. Douglas: 'Environmental sampling in Redcliffe Street', 1982-83 (on plant remains), R.H. Jones: 'Excavations at 68-72 Redcliffe Street, 1982' (i.e. next to gate) both in *Bristol and Avon Archaeology II* (1983)

R.H. Jones: *Canynges House: Survey and Excavations 1983-84* (City of Bristol Museum and Art Gallery, 1984)

J. Jones and N. Watson: *The Early Medieval Waterfront at Redcliffe, Bristol: A Study of Environment and Economy* (British Archaeological Reports (Oxford, 1985))

The latest summary and interpretation of the origins of the city is,

M. Ponsford: 'Bristol' in M. Aston and R. Iles: *The Archaeology of Avon* (1987), pp 145-161.

2

THE FIRST CHURCH:
EARLY ENGLISH

England had been covered with new churches big and small, mainly between 1150 and 1250, after which it was largely a matter of pulling down and rebuilding them.

E. Smith, O. Cook & G. Hutton:
English Parish Churches (1976)

It is certain that the earliest church of St. Mary Redcliffe of which we have visible remains was a building of considerable size and of fine quality workmanship. In Bristol there is good Early English work especially in St. Philip and James, in St. Mark's (the Lord Mayor's Chapel) and in St. Augustine's Abbey, now the Cathedral, as well in the surviving parts of Black Friars (now Quakers Friars) and at St. Bartholomew's Hospital. Masons in Bristol had great expertise not only in the carving of foliage capitals but also in the construction of the newly-invented rib-vaulting. It has been suggested, very appropriately, that Early English St. Mary Redcliffe may well have been a church of the scale and character of the splendid church at New Shoreham, Sussex, and if this was so, it would from the outset have been a building of great grandeur.

Evidence for the major parts of the earliest church on the site of St. Mary Redcliffe is unfortunately very meagre. In his *Notes on the Church* (1878) J.P. Norris, the vicar, records the discovery during recent restoration work of five 'worked stones': these he listed in *Some Account of the Church of St. Mary Redcliffe* (1882) as being in the Mede Monument. Several years ago the present author noted seeing fragments of Late Romanesque or Transitional carving - pieces of zig-zag moulding and a pair of highly developed trumpet capitals - on the wall-bench in the north transept. But in 1985 these could not, alas, be found in spite of repeated searches and requests.

A relatively secure date, about 1190, is connected with the oldest of Redcliffe commemorations, the grant by Robert, Lord of Berkeley, of his Ruge Well, the local water conduit.

The most significant and earliest part of the original church to survive is the inner north porch, Early English work of fine quality. The most obvious feature is its 'purbeck style' which had become dominant in England since the rebuilding of the east end of Canterbury following the fire of 1174. The major early example locally of the marble shafted style is the Lady Chapel at Glastonbury Abbey, built after a fire in 1186. Brakspear (1922) and others suggest a date of c. 1190-1200 for the work at St. Mary Redcliffe, making it very precocious: the chapel at Glastonbury is in a Transitional style with many Romanesque features whereas the inner north porch is confidently Gothic. Salisbury, it will be recalled, was begun in 1220. In Bristol, the Elder Lady Chapel of St. Augustine's Abbey, now the Cathedral, dates from the same decade: the carvings here are documented and related to the earlier campaigns at Wells. But the capitals of the inner north porch are very deeply

The inner north porch. Watercolour by James Johnson, 1828.
Braikenridge Collection, City Art Gallery. *The doorway*
into the church was later altered by the Victorians.

undercut and wind-blown, and bear comparison with those of the west end of the nave at Wells, of nearer 1230.

The entry to the porch from the quayside is through a very impressive Gothic arch of 5 + 7 + 5 rolls, the hollows between them still showing specks of red paint. This arch is supported by a cluster of separate shafts of the local substitute for Purbeck marble, blue lias; the shafts are arranged two (one missing), two, and a group of three in triplet form. The bases are of the 'water-holding' variety, concentrically moulded. The capitals are of boldly undercut 'wind-blown' stiff leaf, a little rough and bold rather than crisp and fine. Above these leaves, the abaci are polygonal with a succession of mouldings which echo those of the bases. This work is carried out very confidently.

Early English capitals and bases, interior north porch,
drawn by George Pryce 1852.

Within the porch the side walls have a plinth or seat with a chamfered top edge: on this rest concentric bases for the 'marble' columns. The capitals at the top of these columns, with the exception of those next to the south wall which are plainly moulded , are again of a deep-cut stiff leaf pattern of a wind-blown variety. Above the abaci which have deeply cut hollows are the wall arches which also have deeply cut hollows. The cumulative effect of plain cylinders of dark 'marble' set in stone so deeply carved is still very splendid: when originally picked out in colour, probably blue and red with gold, the impact would have been strong and vigorous.

There seems to have been a little hesitation in the placing of the vault. The two eastern capitals are rather coarse and plain while the two western ones, though of foliage, are not in the same style as those below, either in the great entry arch or on the blank arcading of the side walls. But the vault itself is neatly and precisely detailed with the fillet on the mouldings of the wall-arches being repeated at either side of the broad flat central moulding of the diagonal ribs. In the centre of the vault is a pretty stiff leaf boss, probably restored and certainly regilded. It looks insubstantial in comparison with the rich growth of the Late Gothic bosses which decorate the vaults inside the church.

From the outer north porch can be seen the window in the original exterior gable of the Early English porch. It is of plate tracery, with a pair of trefoil-headed lancets beneath a quatrefoil, enclosed by a hood-mould with endstops in the form of the heads of a king and a queen. The original porch may well have looked like that of the church of the Hospital of St. Cross at Winchester , a work of the same decades.

The inner, south, wall of the porch with the door leading into the church is now fourteenth century in appearance and was accepted as such by Professor Pevsner in his description of the church for his *Buildings of England* series. But in truth all the detail of the wall is 'restoration' work, as is proven by the watercolour in the Braikenridge Collection.

The dating of the Early English church is not perhaps a matter of great significance since so little survives. But Barrett's listing of records of repairs to the church in 1207, 1229 and 1230 have been usually repeated by later writers.

Barrett also recorded - from material, he says, from Canynges' chest in the room over the north porch (and no doubt passed on to him by Chatterton) - indulgences which relate to the fabric of the church: 1232 for Helen Wedmore, granted by Bishop John of Ardfert; 1246 granted by David, Archbishop of Cashel: this one is quoted in Latin by Barrett; 1246 granted by Christian, 'Episcopus Hymelacensis', another of 1278 granted by Robert, Bishop of Bath and Wells; one of 1287 granted by Peter Quivil, Bishop of Exeter.

Brakspear in his major article (1922) suggested that the original St. Mary Redcliffe may have been cruciform in plan with a central tower, like several other major churches in the area. That St. Mary Redcliffe

*The tower arch into the north nave aisle before alteration. Watercolour by
James Johnson, 1828.* Braikenridge Collection, City Art Gallery.

had aisles to its nave even in the Early English period is indicated by the position of the inner north porch; it abuts on to the present aisle rather than being enclosed within it.

Subsequently, probably in the latter part of the thirteenth century, the present tower was begun. Its position is eccentric, especially as it seems unlikely that there was ever any intention of creating a twin-towered facade. Its asymmetrical form is very noticeable from the west, with buttresses and extra pinnacles to the north and west on the sides away from the body of the church.

From the churchyard it is still possible to get an impression of how the building rises from the rocky cliff. The foundations of the tower were explored in 1870, before the present spire was built - a drawing is included as an appendix to Norris' article of 1878 - and even now one can see how uneven everything is. Something odd has happened to the lowest part of the west wall where the stub of a redundant buttress still survives; perhaps the window above it was widened after the wall had been built.

The tracery of the two windows of the tower is not inconsistent with the character of the richly moulded enclosing arches and deeply sloping sills, but the present tracery, though in a style current in about 1280, is in fact the work of the Victorian restorers. In the Restoration Appeal pamphlet issued in 1842 are the ominous words 'We propose to alter the windows of the Tower, from their present forms and proportions, to others, more in character with the design of the superstructure.'

Inside the tower the whole impact of the space beneath it has been most severely altered by the insertion of the pretty but spider's web Perpendicular lierne vault just above the line of an Early English moulding. Other significant alterations were also made by the Victorians as they sought to strengthen the tower to support the spire: previously the space under the tower must have been much more open, now it is very much cut off from the main body of the church. The great arch southwards towards the nave has been considerably narrowed and similarly, though less obviously, the arch eastwards into the north nave aisle was strengthened by the addition of masonry to form bases, shafts and capitals (probably on original lines). The earlier, unrestored and more open form of this eastern archway is recorded in a watercolour in the Braikenridge Collection (M1950). The lack of any coloured marble shafts is in complete contrast with the work in the immediately preceding, yet adjoining, inner north porch and indicates a change in masons.

Higher up in the tower there are other puzzles, particularly noticeable to those who have the opportunity of climbing up on the roof of the north nave aisle. The walls of the Early English parts of the tower do not appear to survive to equal height. Perhaps the tower was not brought to completion at this period, or possibly its upper parts were at some later date damaged. There are still obvious indications that the exterior of the west wall of the church is equally chequered in its history: at some time, as the unequal height of the buttresses show, it seems to have been heightened. Inside the ringing chamber a mark along the walls was interpreted by Brakspear as being a sign that a lead roof was built, suggesting a more than temporary interruption to the work.

The evidence for the character of the main vessel of the church, though slight, is sufficient for relatively firm conclusions to be made.

At the west end of the nave on the wall adjoining the tower are clear signs in the masonry of the form of two bays of ribbed vaulting. This rose to about 40 feet above the floor from a polygonal capital corbelled out a little precariously on stiff-leaf foliage capitals above a set of triplets. In form the vault must have looked very much like that built over the nave of Gloucester Cathedral in about 1240.

Fragment of Early English clerestory.

On the outside of the same wall, again visible from the roof of the north porch, are the remains of a nook shaft of the same date, and perhaps part of a corbelled parapet. This was illustrated by Norris in his article (1878), and is frequently reproduced in later guidebooks.

George Pryce, in 1853, recorded that '... in the present restoration of the structure it became necessary to remove part of the exterior wall on the north side of the chancel, between the clerestory windows and the parapet; in doing which portions of Early English columns were discovered, the reverse side of which was wrought into Perpendicular English panelling...'

The implication seems to be that the Early English church had a clerestory throughout its length. Another deduction can also be proposed, that the present late medieval church was developed by *remodelling*, not just by adding new parts to a smaller existing structure.

Brakspear's plan of the church - a copy of which hangs at the west end of the church - shows the core of the west wall as being Early English and contemporary with the inner north porch. The wall is very thick and encloses within it a vice giving access to a walk-way at the foot of the great west window and ultimately to the belfry. The thickness of the wall also shows on the exterior at the south west corner of the church where there is a pair of buttresses at the end of the aisle to accommodate its great weight .

That the west wall should be considered in this context is further emphasised by the form of the window at the end of the south aisle. This has a two-centred arch like the windows in the tower, but the mouldings of the arch are not the same: on the inside the form is reminiscent of the eastern windows of the Berkeley Chapel in the Cathedral. The tracery also is different from that in the tower for below the 3-, 4- and 6-foiled forms at the top of the window each light is headed by a 5-foil ogee arch, bending in an S form. Ogee arches are one of the features which characterise Decorated rather than Early English; but probably not too much ought to be read into this, as tracery seems to have invited restorers to display their scholarship and inventiveness. From the exterior one can see how the essential unity of the west wall of the church is emphasised by the form of the buttresses of the tower and to either side of the great west door: all are to the same pattern with little shafts at the corners. But the two buttresses of the west wall of the tower do not rise so high as that at the end of the south arcade of the nave: as already noticed, the wall has been a good deal adapted at its upper levels.

Effigy of a knight: late thirteenth century, now in north transept.
Photo: *Damian Gillie.*

Architectural mouldings and tracery patterns, though aesthetically pleasing, are rather arid in terms of human interest. The character of Early English man - if we may, like archaeologists, speak in such a fashion - is more evident in the art of his funeral monuments. Of these some beautiful examples survive in the church.

The first to be considered must be the slab-fragments found during the course of the Victorian restoration and now collected together in the chapel within the tower. In the churchyard outside are stone coffins which may perhaps be related to them. All four slabs are carved with crosses, with foliate elements. Though now battered and broken, they were once very elegant.

The over life-size effigy of a knight is a very grand piece of sculpture and even though battered it is still romantic in its impact. Its present position, on a plain plinth, tucked away in the north east corner of the north transept, is unfortunate.

The knight is shown wearing a complete suit of chain-mail, covering an iron skull-cap, as well as the hands and feet: there is no plate armour. Over the mail is worn a long flowing surcoat which might once have been coloured. On the left arm is a damaged heater-shaped shield, and though the knight is shown with eyes apparently closed and his head resting on two cushions, he has his hands engaged in sheathing his sword. His legs are outstretched, and quietly crossed; on his ankles are spurs; his feet rest on the traditional dog, fawning like a pet labrador. The effigy has been trimmed: the right elbow and lower part of the shield are missing, and at some time, legs have been broken. Nor has the nose escaped mutilation.

The effigy is one of a small but inter-related group in Bristol. At SS. Philip and Jacob is the head of a similar knight and at the Lord Mayor's Chapel are two excellent (and more three-dimensional) cross-legged knights always presumed to represent the founder of St. Mark's, Maurice de Gaunt, died 1220, and his nephew and heir, Robert de Gournay, died 1269. Such effigies, and there are many more in the Bristol area, remind us of the age of castles, Goodrich in Herefordshire being one of the finest of the period to survive, and of the military temper of the period. Bristol Castle, once so important, has long ago almost entirely disappeared.

The Redcliffe knight is clearly not in its correct position: in 1813 Britton recorded it in the western aisle of the transept. The tradition that the figure represents Robert II, 3rd Lord Berkeley who died in 1220, can be traced back to Barrett's *History and Antiquities of Bristol* of 1789.

George Pryce in *History of Bristol* (1861) suggested that the monument may have been moved from the hospital of St. Catherine which was dissolved in 1549, of which foundation Robert was a considerable benefactor who was commemorated annually. These suggestions for so early a date, accepted by Roper, have by now been refuted.

Anderson emphasises the roughness of the carving of the Redcliffe knight. He also points out that the double-cushion under the head seems not to appear in England as early as 1220 but for the first time on the bronze effigies of King Henry III and of Queen Eleanor (died 1290) and on the tomb of Aveline, Countess of Lancaster, all in Westminster Abbey, and that all the evidence points towards a date 'towards the end of the century'. The effigy may well have been ordered years after the death of the knight with whom by tradition it is usually identified.

Dating effigies and trying to identify them with named individuals is notoriously difficult. In general terms, the next development of armour is represented by the two early fourteenth century Berkeley Knights in the south choir aisle of St. Augustine's Abbey, now Bristol Cathedral, whose armour shows the first phases of the transition towards plate armour. The context alters from the crusades to the battles of the Hundred Years War.

What then can be deduced about the Early English Church on Redcliffe Hill? The impression is of a major church with considerable architectural pretensions, dominating the quayside. By the end of the thirteenth century Bristol was still growing in importance, and the port's increasing prosperity was to find its most lasting expression in the further enrichment of St. Mary Redcliffe.

FURTHER READING

Pamphlet: *St. Mary Redcliffe Pipe Walk, 1190-1990: A Souvenir Booklet to commemorate the 800th Anniversary of the Redcliffe Water Supply* (1990)

The following two books supplement each other:

I.M. Roper: *The Monumental Effigies of Gloucestershire and Bristol* (Gloucester, 1931)

A.C. Fryer: *Monumental Effigies in Somerset* (Reprinted from *Proceedings of the Somerset Archaeological and Natural History Society*, 1932)

For a specialist survey,

A. Anderson: *English Influence in Norwegian and Swedish Figure Sculpture in Wood, 1220-1270* (Stockholm, 1950), esp. p.51.

Two of the early slabs are illustrated, less damaged, in J.F. Nicholas and J. Taylor: *Bristol, Past and Present* (1881), vol. II.

In about 1250 a chapel of the Holy Spirit was erected to the south west of the church. After serving for some time as a Free School it was demolished in 1763. Its plan is reproduced in E. Williams : *The Chantries of William Canynges* (1950), p123.

3

DECORATED:
THE OUTER NORTH PORCH

There are buttresses, machicolations, and turrets, and the architecture is perverse and fantastic in the extreme.

E.W. Meyerstein: *A Life of Chatterton* (1930)

Magnificent porches are a major feature of many of the churches of England. One of the most spectacular, from the Romanesque period, is that of Malmesbury Abbey. The double-storeyed Early English porch of St. Mary Redcliffe provided the major entry into the church, a major architectural feature dominating the quayside and inviting all who approached from the centre of Bristol.

Such porches built on the sides of churches and facing towards the centre of population retained their popularity throughout the Middle Ages. Frequently, as in the Early English period at Wells and Salisbury, in the Decorated period at Hereford and in the Perpendicular at Gloucester, Worcester and Canterbury, side porches vied in importance with the doorways in the centre of the west front. The culmination of this fashion, which is entirely dominant in parish church architecture, is the prodigious porch at Cirencester.

Many earlier writers have dated the outer part of the north porch at St. Mary Redcliffe as early as c. 1290: all modern authorities agree that c. 1320 would be a more acceptable date. Whatever its date, the outer north porch at St. Mary Redcliffe is outstanding both for its architectural form and for the exuberance of its sculptured decoration. Its dominance is such that most visitors hardly notice the fine Early English porch against which it was built.

The approach up a flight of steps to the main door of the porch has been altered several times, particularly about half a century ago with the construction of the new domestic rooms in their hornworks. The siting of the church on the slope of the hill means that the north porch must always have been impressively set, high above the level of the quayside.

The immediate precedents for the form of the outer north porch must have been the series of crosses erected to the memory of Queen Eleanor who had died in 1290. Both Waltham Cross and Charing Cross - the latter now replaced by a splendid Victorian essay - were hexagonal, as is the porch. But the link with the Eleanor crosses, including the triangular one at Geddington and the octagonal one at Hardingstone, is in the richness of spectacularly ornamental carving as well as in their plans and elevations.

Whether the north porch was originally planned to have a spire like the Eleanor crosses is uncertain but improbable, for it is squeezed somewhat uncomfortably against the great north west tower on which a very tall spire rises so dominantly. There was early in the fourteenth century a new fashion in the west country, as at the Chapter House at Wells, for buildings to have flat, drum-like tops.

The great doorway at the top of the steps is so inviting that it is easy to rush in without exploring the exterior of the porch, but it deserves attention, even though all the carving is now entirely re-cut.

The exterior of the porch is unified by the dominant verticals of the massive polygonal buttresses. These are adorned with extravagantly modelled niches for statuary: the recurrence of so many ogees and nodding ogees bulging out from beneath gables indicates that the work can be properly compared to the contemporary work around the walls of the magnificent Lady Chapel at Ely Cathedral. There may indeed be connections with Ely also in the detail, especially in the sculptures of the crouching figures who pretend to support the pedestals for the missing, or restored, statuary. Equally lively figures also survive at the doorway from the south transept into the south choir ambulatory at Gloucester.

Midway up the porch the band of niches provides a strong horizontal band around the whole structure. The effect is weakened by the loss of the original statuary which once filled every niche.

At the top of the porch a circuit of very small windows provides light for an upper room, one of the most romantic literary sites in the whole length of Britain, the Treasury or 'Chatterton's Room' - the significance of which will be more fully discussed in a subsequent chapter.

By now all the stonework of the exterior of the porch has been renewed, some as recently as 1987. The statues of SS. Augustine and Anselm, of the Annunciation over the main door, of St. Ambrose and Bishop Cornish date from the restoration of the 1930s and were carved by A.G. Walker, A.R.A. Several of the original carvings from beneath the pedestals for statues are to be discovered scattered haphazardly around the inside of the church. There are few pieces of sculpture of any period in Bristol displaying such vigour and character: they are work of great quality. The marvellously complex and contorted poses are entirely characteristic of this most lively phase of English art. Though some of the figures are using crutches, and may represent maimed pilgrims, there seems to be no coherent programme. Suggestions have been made that some of the smaller sculptures indicate that the porch could have served as a Sacrament House or Holy Sepulchre.

Quite clearly the outer north porch is not just a way into the church: it is a distinct architectural and sculptural experience. Each part deserves

Outer north porch, c.1320. Engraving from John Britton, 1813.

Supporting figure from outer north porch, now in north choir aisle.

unhurried attention. As the worshipper approaches the main doorway of the porch he finds another door ahead of him, beyond the steps up into the inner Early English porch. But the outer north porch turns out to be an exciting place to be in, with the walls set unexpectedly all at angles, with a recessed shrine to the right. Usually it is furnished simply with a Crucifix, but at Christmas it serves happily as the setting for a crib. If one looks into this shrine, one can see how the porch is angled in next the lowest part of the buttress of the great tower.

The pilgrim to this shrine was not necessarily directed by the form of the outer porch into the main body of the church: left and right, towards south east and north west are minor doorways. Presumably the patrons and the architect wished to provide a structure through which devotees to the shrine could pass easily, quickly and informally.

Vault of outer north porch, with facade of the Early English inner porch.
Photo: *Damian Gillie.*

Interior of outer north porch from the inner porch. Watercolour by James Johnson, 1828. Braikenridge Collection, City Art Gallery.

The shrine - for that is what the outer porch was built as - could function without any disturbance to the rest of the church, and the pilgrim could easily offer a last prayer before hurrying across the quay to his ship. There is documentary evidence, in William Worcestre, which supports this interpretation, and other evidence, more ambiguously, in Bristol wills. Probably one should imagine a statue, surrounded by lamps and candles, and even an *ex voto* (perhaps many) in the shape of a ship.

The interior of the outer porch is very high and airy - much taller than the inner, Early English porch - with an internal walkway passing through the thickness of the buttresses. The windows are generously proportioned with three lights: at the top, the tracery is extremely relaxed with a very wide-open multifoil dominant. The lower parts of the lights are tapered into a dagger-like form, while the mullions descend to the level of the walkway forming a regular blank panelling which foreshadows the forms so dominant in the Perpendicular style - in an early form in the south transept of Gloucester, c. 1330, and later in a mature form around most of the latter parts of St. Mary Redcliffe itself.

The series of faces which punctuate the hollow moulded around the middle of the wall are of fine quality and, though smaller, quite similar to those on the vault supports over the aisles in the cathedral.

The most magical effect of the interior of the porch is achieved by the way in which the gigantic buttresses, so dominant on the exterior, are reduced to a wedge in the interior; from the narrowest parts of these spring the twenty four ribs of the vault.

At the top-centre, the ribs cross to form a hexagon the angles of which point toward the apex of each window rather than to each buttress: the central hexagon of ribs thus seems to spin in relation to its supports. The same conventions, the same sense of fun, can be seen in the vault of the Chapter House at Wells Cathedral and more pertinently, without any central support, in the Lady Chapel of the same church. This is English Gothic at its most enjoyable and vivacious.

The outer north porch is a building of such a capricious design that the identification of the various sources of inspiration is of great interest. As we have seen, the context of the inner part of the north porch is the earliest phase of Early English. For the outer part of the porch, the immediate local context is that of work at Wells Cathedral, particularly the Chapter House and Lady Chapel (1307 and 1326). There are also a few elements which seem to lead towards the earliest work in the novel Perpendicular style in the south transept at Gloucester. Several features seem to relate also to Decorated work in the Lady Chapel at Ely Cathedral, again foreshadowing the Perpendicular.

Close connections (which will be noted again in the next phase of the rebuilding of St. Mary Redcliffe) also exist with the work built by the eccentric genius responsible for the design of the new choir arm, 1298, of St. Augustine's Abbey, now Bristol Cathedral. One particular feature, though tiny, which indicates this link is the design of the miniature vaults in the niches with nodding ogees at either side of the archway between the outer and inner north porches: these echo those of the choir aisles in the Cathedral. Similarly, the use of 'Berkeley arches', most easily recognisable at the door to the stairs to the upper rooms, indicates another connection with the Cathedral.

Professor Pevsner in his description (1958) of these buildings refers to the influence of oriental art, both Indian and Chinese: 'Historically that is possible since Bristol was one of England's busiest ports.' These ideas can be explored only briefly here in an attempt to explain how a Bristol architect could have learned the elements of oriental design. We can support generalities with selected instances.

It is clear that the polygonal form of the outer north porch (and of the Eleanor crosses) is not classical in inspiration: but polygonal shapes are dominant in Islamic art and architecture. The origin of the ogee arch is to be sought in northern India in the third century B.C. The multifoiled arch of the main door, like the tomb recesses in the south nave aisle (and in the Cathedral), are reminiscent of Chinese art from as early as the third-fourth century A.D. The ornate frame of the main doorway suggests the luxuriance of Seljuk portals in Asia Minor or the stucco-work of Islamic Spain.

Contacts between Britain and the Near East were frequent throughout the Middle Ages: pilgrims and crusaders travelled to the Holy Land, merchants traded around the Mediterranean. Bristol ships reached Spain regularly: in that country Moorish influence was all-pervasive, and the markets of southern Spain were famous for their luxury goods imported from all parts of Asia. It was not only wine which Bristol imported; many shiploads of pilgrims are closely documented as they made their regular pilgrimages to the shrine of St. James at Santiago, and doubtless these pilgrims (like their present-day successors) brought back mementoes - an ivory or a bowl, leather or glass or pottery decorated with Islamic or Mozarabic designs.

Skelton engraving of the outer north porch, from John Britton, 1813.

We need to remember the trading contacts into the Mediterranean, particularly with Pisa, and with Genoa and Venice, great maritime powers with depots not only at Byzantium but also in the Black Sea, notably in Trebizond and in the Crimea. Italian merchants traded westward, carrying goods to London, Sandwich and Southampton; occasionally their ships reached the Severn. The cloth trade relied on Italian merchants to bring them the famous red dye, granum, from Portugal; the mordant used to fix such dyes came from the Black Sea. It has been suggested that the fragments of enamelled glass, made probably in Egypt but found in Westminster Abbey and at Abingdon, had been imported by Venetian merchants. The most spectacular survival of this sort of luxury item is the Luck of Edenhall (now in The Victoria and Albert Museum), a slender beaker enamelled with red, white, blue and green: it dates from the mid thirteenth century, the period of the later crusades in which English knights played their part.

Evidence of trading contacts with Islamic land is nowhere as clear anywhere in England as it is in Pisa where many of the Romanesque churches were decorated with chargers, deep broad-rimmed bowls, brought back from all around the Mediterranean shore, from Moorish Spain, from Morocco, North Africa, Egypt and the Levant. But archaeologists working at Grosmont Castle have found a fragment of a blue glazed pot made at Rakka in Syria.

Oriental designs travel well on pottery, and survive well - better than they do on perishable goods. At Bodmin, the relics of St. Petroc are in an ivory casket made and decorated by a Muslim, probably in Sicily. At Westminster the relics of St. Edward the Confessor were wrapped, like those of many another saint, in rich and rare fabrics with oriental designs. The connections are right across Asia along the Silk Route towards China.

It was not only pilgrims, crusaders and traders who travelled to the Near East. Adelard of Bath travelled to Salerno, to Sicily and to the Levant in c.1114-c.1120: his knowledge of Euclid, through Arabic sources, and of eastern architecture, notably the construction of great arches for bridges, and of astronomy is well attested. Half a century later than this, the Great Gateway of St. Augustine's (now the Cathedral) on College Green is designed in a manner reminiscent of Syrian work, though it does not look quite so Islamic as does the main door of another Augustinian house, Kenilworth. Though (to use John Harvey's phrase) the story of the Saracen mason, Lalys, 'may have been improved by legendary embroidery', a record of his work in South

Wales and for Henry I seems acceptable as evidence of direct personal knowledge of Islamic architecture in Britain.

In the thirteenth century, as the political situation altered, knowledge of the art and culture further eastward - especially from Central Asia and China - reached Europe as missionaries and embassies made their famous journeys, notably the Franciscan Giovanni di Piano del Carpine in 1246, William Rubruck of Bruges in 1254, and Maffeo, Niccolo and Marco Polo in 1269-72 and 1275-91. Edward I had many contacts with the Ilkhan Mongols of Persia (whose art at this period was much influenced by the art of China) from the time of his alliance with them during his siege of Acre in 1271. Later two Mongol embassies visited him in Gascony, and the king sent his own, led by Sir Geoffrey de Langley, via Trebizond to Tabriz in 1291-92. For this journey detailed expense accounts survive, including records of the purchase of art-works, a Tartar cup, silver, two painted dishes, carpets, clothing, any of which could have influenced craftsmen in England. Among those named in the accounts is Robert the Sculptor. Records of this journey validate the comparison made by Prof. Bony (*The English Decorated Style*, p.49) between the vault of the Lady Chapel at Wells and vault 47 of the Masjid Camii at Isfahan. Sir Geoffrey de Langley's party, Robert the Sculptor among them, saw similar buildings which could have provided inspiration for the design and detailing of the north porch.

One piece of corroborative evidence must be mentioned. Bound up in a single volume (Corpus Christi College, Cambridge ms. 407) with copies of the journeys of William de Rubruck and of another great missionary traveller to China, Odoric of Pordenone, is the unique surviving copy of *Liber Itinerarium* - the narrative of a journey to the Holy Land in 1322-23 made by two Irish Franciscans, Simon Simeon and (note the name) Hugh the Illuminator. A great part of the narrative is a description of Alexandria and Cairo (where Hugh died of dysentery).

As John Harvey has pointed out, the design used for the tracery in the south walk (c.1324) of the cloister at Norwich - work by William Ramsey - is predated by similar forms used for the Mausoleum of Mustafa Pasha (1269-73) in Cairo. Interestingly, the *Liber Itinerarium* manuscript now in Cambridge was owned by Simon Bozoun, Prior of Norwich Cathedral, 1344-52. And as he sat in his prior's stall he would have used the Ormesby Psalter (Bodleian ms. Douce 366) which is famed for the decorations of its borders, work of c. 1320. In the corners of many of the borders are complex inter-laced patterns for which precedents must be sought in Islamic, and particularly Seljuk art.

In St. Mary Redcliffe similar sorts of patterns are used for six of the roundels of ancient glass now in the north window of the tower. Comparable with these, though not quite identical, are the designs on a silk cloth now in The Victoria and Albert Museum, fourteenth or fifteenth century work from Moorish Spain or North Africa: it was once used as a hanging behind a statue of the Virgin in a church in Florence. Perhaps the Virgin of Redcliffe was similarly honoured with a thank-offering, given by a merchant safely returned to port, unloading his ship at the quay below the north porch.

The north porch is a key monument in a crucial phase of English architecture. It is disappointing that we cannot suggest a name for its architect, though all recent authorities agree that there is a connection with lost work at St. Paul's and at Westminster, and with the work of the Ramsey family at Norwich, Ely and in the novel Perpendicular remodelling of Gloucester.

The porch has no progeny in England. Though there are hexagonal porches at Chipping Norton and at Ludlow, these bear no comparison. But many travellers have suggested that the outer north porch may have influenced buildings in Spain and Portugal, notably the Capellas Imperfetas at Batalha in Portugal, begun in c.1503. This building is reminiscent of an English octagonal chapter house, while its doors are designed as extravagant versions of the doorways into the outer north porch. The wine trade could have provided the link, for it must be remembered that on any trade route influences can move in both directions.

FURTHER READING

The entrance from the north aisle into the porch is through a frontispiece, perhaps from a screen or pulpitum, with faded inscriptions.

For four of the loose sculptures from the porch, see *The Age of Chivalry* (Royal Academy, 1987) nos. 502-505; see also no. 409 in which Dr. Wilson emphasises the local context of the porch. For the interpretation of grotesque and secular elements as in the carvings, see M. Camille: *Image on the Edge: the margins of medieval art* (1992).

For an analysis of the wider context, see Paul Crossley: 'Wells, the West Country and Central European Late Gothic, in Medieval Art and Architecture at Wells and Glastonbury': *British Archaeological Association Transactions 1978* (1981), pp.81-109.

J. Bony: *The English Decorated Style* (1979) is essential, as is J. Harvey: *English Medieval Architects: A Biographical Dictionary* (revised edition 1986). For the name of an architect at St. Augustine's Abbey (Bristol Cathedral), see A.J. Taylor: 'A petition from Nicholas Derneford to Edward II': *Transactions of Bristol and Glos. Archaeological Society XCVIII* (1981).

For the connections with the Orient, J. Harvey: *The Master Builders* (1971), esp. pp. 80-95. See also I. de Rachewitz: *Papal Envoys to the Great Khans* (1971); C. Desimoni: 'I Conti dell'Ambasciata al Chan di Persia in 1292': *Atti Liguri di Storia Patria* (Genoa, 1877-84), pp. 537-698; M. Esposito: 'Itinerarium Symonis Semeonis Ab Hybernia Ad Terram Sanctam': *Scriptores Latini Hiberniae IV* (Dublin, 1960).

It would be impertinent to attempt a bibliography of archaeological evidence of Islamic imports, so only a few examples are mentioned. For Rakka ware, see J.M. Lewis: *Medieval Pottery and Metal-ware in Wales*, National Museum of Wales, 1978; M. Wenzel: 'Thirteenth Century Enamelled Glass found in Medieval Abingdon': *Oxford Journal of Archaeology 3.3.* (Nov. 1984). Hispano-Moresque lustre pottery has been found recently in the Deansway excavations at Worcester (where the Cathedral Library still holds several books of Islamic science): compare similar material illustrated in E.J. Boore: *Excavations at Tower Lane, Bristol*, City of Bristol Museum and Art Gallery (1984).

For an excellent survey, see the catalogue: *The Art of Islam* (The Arts Council, 1976), e.g. no.18.

4

DECORATED:
THE CHURCH REMODELLED

... every building of the Gothic period differs in some respect from every other ... pointed arches do not constitute Gothic, nor vaulted roofs, nor flying buttresses, nor grotesque sculptures: but all or some of these things, and many other things with them, when they come together so as to have life.

John Ruskin *The Stones of Venice* (1851):
The Nature of Gothic

The early fourteenth century was the Golden Age of British art. Nowhere is this term more appropriate than in the west of England where so many of its greatest churches were extensively remodelled, enlarged or rebuilt. All this work cost a vast amount of money, but for most of the buildings records do not on the whole survive to allow a full analysis. Doubtless much work was done at the request and expense of those wealthy families whose coats of arms appear so prominently in many parts of the buildings. The history of these families, some of the most powerful in the whole country, was often troubled, and it must be expected that the changing fortunes of the patrons are reflected in the history of the buildings with which they were involved.

The frequently violent commotions of the times must have affected, if even only spasmodically, all levels of society in Bristol - merchants and clergy as well as masons. Later in its history the fate of the church has been influenced to varying extents by such events as the Napoleonic and Crimean Wars, and even recent crises in the Middle East. Bristol was a refuge for Edward II during his flight in October 1326 and perhaps again in his temporary escape from custody in July 1327. It was while in the custody of Thomas Berkeley, one of the family so closely related, as patrons, to St. Augustine's Abbey, now Bristol Cathedral, that Edward II was murdered. The king's body found rest in a marvellous shrine-like tomb in the choir at St. Peter's Abbey, now the cathedral, at Gloucester: whether this burial and the birth of Perpendicular are inter-related or coincidental is still disputed. But it is clear that political catastrophes did have their effect on other buildings in the west country. Of the king's supporters, the Despenser family who were responsible for the remodelling of Tewkesbury Abbey, suffered greatly: Hugh Despenser the Elder was hanged at Bristol on October 9th 1326 and his son, Hugh the Younger, was executed at Hereford on October 29th. Their assiduously acquired great estates, including those around St. Mary Redcliffe, were dispersed.

At this time Exeter Cathedral was being entirely rebuilt, but work was interrupted when its bishop, Walter de Stapledon, was set upon by the mob and beheaded on October 15th 1326.

Within a working lifetime of these events there occurred an even more frightening disaster. Whatever work was in progress on the rebuilding of St. Mary Redcliffe must no doubt have been at least temporarily interrupted by the events surrounding the deposition of Edward II; yet such interruptions would have been relatively minor compared to those caused by the Black Death. There may well have been thirty five to forty per cent mortality in Bristol.

It is easy to forget how a sequence of catastrophes must have affected the progress of work on St. Mary Redcliffe. So grand an undertaking as the remodelling of a large church is not to be measured as the work of a single season or decade. St. Mary Redcliffe was built and rebuilt with the use of the very simplest of mechanical aids, and through many lifetimes of craftsmen and patrons.

Nevertheless the overall unity of design of the late medieval church which we see today is such that we can be quite certain that the main design dates from the early fourteenth century. The original forms could not have been much departed from without disrupting the stability of the whole structure, though details of wall design, window tracery and vault pattern were altered to suit the changes that took place, perhaps following the replacement of a master mason, developments in the current style of architecture, or simply fashion.

The major feature which makes St. Mary Redcliffe such a spectacular success was the planning of transepts with aisles both to east and west: these give an architectural grandeur which is not to be found in many a major cathedral or abbey. But before we deal with these we must begin, as did the masons, with the rebuilding of the south nave aisle. It has been accepted that the Early English church had transepts: presumably, from early in the fourteenth century, the plan was to remodel them once the south nave aisle had been rebuilt. The width of the nave can be presumed as that of the Early English church.

One easily overlooked element in the design of the new church would have been more visible in the middle ages and more significant: the bench which runs round the whole of the interior of the outer wall of the main body of the church. Nowadays it is mostly obscured by the Victorian heating pipes and pews. The bench begins in the western bays of the south nave aisle as a plain right-angled step, but then continues in a slightly richer form, with a ledge at the top at the eastern end of the south nave aisle, as can be seen, too, in the south transept and thence all round the church. As in the north porch of the church this provides a simple but effective continuous feature binding the building both structurally and visually into a unified composition.

The bench round the outer wall is interrupted in three bays of the south nave aisle to allow for the three extraordinary tomb recesses, quite dramatic essays in the most capricious Decorated style. The recesses are

56

The south side of the nave with its aisle and the
south transept, showing building breaks.

so important a feature of the design that they must have been intended to house the tombs for major patrons of the new work. Comparison may be made with the equally grand tomb recesses created at about this period as part of the chantry foundations for the Alard and Farncombe families in Winchelsea.

The recesses were rediscovered in 1852 during the Victorian restoration of the church. George Pryce recorded that all the carving had been greatly damaged, 'the walls rendered quite flat to make way for the unsightly wooden partitions which separate the rich from their poorer fellow-worshippers.' A somewhat similar tomb recess was discovered at about the same date in the north aisle of St. Stephen's church in the centre of Bristol, and has similarly been restored by Victorian stone-carvers.

Many writers have taken it for granted that the design for the tomb recesses was derived from St. Augustine's Abbey, now Bristol Cathedral. But the tomb recesses in the Cathedral have a polygonal inner frame while in St. Mary Redcliffe the geometry of the outer exploding ogee curves - with their crocketing and massy foliage as well as the swinging curves of the inner moulding, and another ogee curving down to form a hanging pendant - is all much more wilful. It is as rich as anything in the wildest Seljuk sculpture. The exuberance of the detail - even though restored - is unrestrained, and the effect is made even more curious in the eastern bay of the aisle where the need to turn the outer wall into the south transept means that the vertical of the central mass of foliage does not coincide with the mullion above.

Essentially the design is oriental in inspiration, but the immediate source is to be found in St. Mary Redcliffe itself, particularly in the designs used for the lesser side entrances into the outer north porch. Here can be seen the same curious pendant ends to the hood moulds which enclose the oval, while at the top is the same extravagant top foliage growth, and a use of ogee curves is the major feature of the inner arch. These details may suggest links with the work of the Ramsey family of architects, as in the lower wall arcading of Ely Lady Chapel, and with the Prior's Door in the cloister at Norwich Cathedral and also in the adjoining book cupboard recesses and a blocked door, which have similar features. What the designer or designers of all these features enjoyed was the swing of one curve against another, and the balancing of a thin linear pattern with the texture of robust foliage carving. Whether the south nave aisle may be attributed to the designer of the outer north porch is uncertain but by no means impossible. A gap of twenty years or so seems not unlikely.

Looking upwards we come next to the windows. We have already seen that the tower has two windows whose form is broad, with a sloping sill and two-centred arches with many mouldings. The same sort of window opening is to be seen in the west wall of the south nave aisle: this window opening was designed to balance that of the west wall of the tower. The effect is most apparent from the exterior, imparting some air of symmetry to the west front. The tracery of this western window of the south aisle may be essentially original: but a plate in the 1842 Restoration Appeal publication shows Perpendicular tracery. As it stands now the tracery is notable for including at the head of each light two-centred or ogee curves - a feature which is characteristic of Decorated. By 1307 ogees were used similarly in the tracery of the windows of Wells Cathedral Chapter House.

Turning to the south wall of the south aisle we find that the arch enclosing the windows is no longer two-centred but four-centred. In later parts of the church, in the transept and choir aisles and in the north aisle of the nave, this form is hardened, though at clerestory level and in the ends of the transepts two-centred forms were retained. Such minor variations do not affect the general unity of the church.

Less noticeable, but indicative of the ways in which different generations of masons could work within the framework of a consistent overall programme, is the variation of mouldings. In the interior of the south nave aisle the mullions have a simple angular pattern but a much more complex profile is used for the subsequent parts of the church.

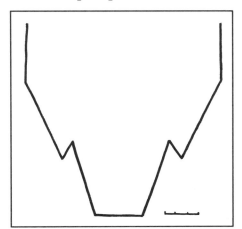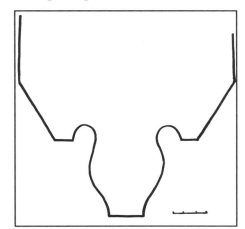

Mouldings of mullions: left: *South nave aisle.* Right: *North nave aisle.*

Furthermore, from the choir aisles onwards - as can easily be seen by comparing the wall of the south nave aisle with that of the north nave aisle - these mullions are produced downwards from the windows to create panelling over the lower wall, a much neater and more unified effect which supersedes the baroque excesses of the exuberantly florid tomb recesses. Panelling is the dominant feature of all the later parts of the church, both on interior and exterior; such panelling is always considered characteristic of Perpendicular: but it can, as has already been noticed, be seen in a precocious form inside the outer north porch.

Window tracery in great churches in the Decorated style is often varied and lively - Exeter Cathedral has a most exciting sequence of designs - but the window tracery for most of St. Mary Redcliffe is now rather repetitive and lacking in variety.

The south nave aisle, of which the structure is distinctively Decorated in character, has Perpendicular tracery: this may be due to interruptions caused by the Black Death, or even Victorian zeal. The adjoining western aisle of the south transept has tracery which includes a not very elegant cusped 'barbed-wire' element which also occurs in the great south window of the transept and in the tracery forms of the south porch. So we may safely presume that the window tracery of the south nave aisle is not in its original form - and its original effect is further altered by the Victorian stained glass.

Around the outer wall and window space of each bay of the south nave aisle is an all-enclosing wall arch with two hollows cut back into it. In front of this is the respond which, visually at least, provides the support for the vault. In essence, its form is a rectangle with hollows cut back into it, and with the corners detailed with a wavy curve; in front as a distinct feature is a triplet cluster of cylindrical shafts, rising to provide visual if not structural support for the vault.

In the church it is easy enough to glance across to the north nave aisle to see how a later generation of masons used a much more integrated and elegant design.

But even in the south nave aisle it is obvious that experiments were going on. Although hidden by the Victorian stalls it is possible to see that along the outer wall the bases of the triplet vaulting shafts rise no higher than knee-level. This height is maintained for the similar detail on the two easternmost piers of the main nave arcade, and also into the south transept. By contrast, the four western piers of the south nave arcade have bases which rise to about waist-level.

There are also minor but significant variations in the proportions and design of the capitals of the vaulting shafts of the south nave aisle. The five westernmost capitals - presumably those of the bays built first - have a long, bare bell shape below a narrow band of foliage. The sixth capital is slightly different but the seventh, at the corner into the south transept, is of a different pattern - with foliage around the bell beneath a concentrically moulded abacus. This form, with minor variations, is thereafter used for the rest of the church.

Much more significant amongst the variations in the overall design of the church is the multiplicity of patterns used for the vaults.

The design of those over the south nave aisle is revolutionary. Where the normal vault - as in the inner north porch - is built upon weight-bearing ribs which form an arch diagonally across the bay, the ribs in the south nave aisle are not visually (nor, probably, structurally) load-bearing. From each corner of the bay rise not one but two ribs. From the peak of the wall-arch, the transverse arches across the bay and from the main nave arcade are seen diamond-shaped patterns, all adorned with cusps. The use of cusped diamonds suggests a connection with the choir vault of St. Augustine's (Bristol Cathedral, from 1298 on), or with the choir and aisles of Wells Cathedral (in progress c.1325-1338). But the totally novel feature is the use in the centre of each bay of the vault of ribs which can have no supporting function for they curve across the surface of the vault.

Similar curved ribs were used subsequently on a much grander scale. In England the major example - which may coincidentally provide a terminus date for the Redcliffe aisle vaults - is to be admired over the choir of Ottery St. Mary, Devon, founded in 1337 by Bishop John Grandisson of Exeter, a great patron of the arts with a wide knowledge of the most fashionable innovations in European art. Probably the architect for Ottery St. Mary was William Joy, the designer of the choir at Wells Cathedral. His influence, if not his hand, may be suspected at Redcliffe during this phase of the rebuilding.

Much later, continental masons, particularly members of the Parler family from Cologne, knew of curved ribs (and also of flying ribs as in the vestibule to the Berkeley Chapel of the Cathedral). Amongst the possible descendants of vaults built in Bristol are those with flying or curved ribs at the cathedrals in Prague and Vienna and in several churches of Bohemia.

The south aisle, then, is a puzzle. Its outer wall with its capriciously designed tomb recesses and the revolutionary vaults are early fourteenth century Decorated work of the most inventive variety. But

Vault of the south nave aisle, showing the curved sides of the central hexagon, c.1330. Photo: Damian Gillie.

the tracery of the aisle windows is in a later, duller, style.

It seems certain that in the early fourteenth century the church still retained its Early English north nave aisle. The major puzzle is the state of the nave aisle. Was the south arcade of the nave (that is to say, the supports for the vault of the south nave aisle) left as Early English work, or remodelled in the Decorated style bay-by-bay as work progressed? Or was the work done even more spasmodically, with the inner face of the south arcade of the nave being remodelled only when the nave itself was transformed into Perpendicular?

The part of St. Mary Redcliffe which can most closely be linked with William Joy's work at Wells is the south porch. It includes new features which seem to affect the character of subsequent parts of the church, notably the detailing of the panelling.

The south porch is clearly in a somewhat curious, altered state. It is known that Victorians moved an exterior stair turret on the east side, but more puzzling are the ambiguities of level between the interior and exterior. From the exterior, the impression is of a rather grand, well-lit single storey structure, with tall windows to east, west (now Victorian work) and south. But on all four walls of the interior are signs which seem to indicate that the vault has been lowered. The ogee mouldings which frame the doorway into the church and the arch from the church yard have both lost their top finials, and the canopy work of the flanking niches is cut off at the top in an awkward, lop-sided manner. Similarly, on the side wall, the central niches are both cut off prematurely.

The way in which the mullions rise perpendicularly and undeflected to the enclosing arch is a novel feature, characteristic of the Perpendicular style. But the other ugly junctions between verticals or gables and the enclosing arches are much more haphazard.

The remodelling of the porch may have been necessitated when the spire fell. Certainly the pattern of the vault is much like that used for the eastern, late, bay of the Lady Chapel, and the change in design is thus likely to date from the fifteenth or even sixteenth century. In the modern masonry, of 1914, of the upper room are two fragments of fifteenth or sixteenth century panelling.

From the outside one can easily recognise that there was a major building break between the south aisle and south transept. The change in design is not just to non-structural features but to the major structural member, the buttress. On the buttresses of the south transept there is a much more complex sequence of mouldings just below window level, and lower a plain wall, whereas the south aisle buttress had two off-sets. It will also be noticed that the windows of the south transept west aisle begin lower than those of the adjoining aisle, and have different enclosing arch and different tracery. Everything is at different levels, and rather a mess.

Even if the Early English church had transepts, it is not certain that they were on the present generous scale. From the north it is quite clear how steeply the hillside falls away, and how the whole northern side of the church is built on a strong masonry platform of late medieval date enclosing an undercroft. The present effect is due in part to the Victorian clearing and levelling of the site but the basic geological situation of the church has not been altered.

Aisled transepts in a parish church are quite unexpected and unusual: only three other parish churches are so furnished, none of them earlier than St. Mary Redcliffe - Melton Mowbray, Leics. (1290-1340), Patrington, Yorks. (1310-1410) and Faversham, Kent (1355-1450). It is the general prestigious character of the new work however, not just one element in the plan, which puts St. Mary Redcliffe firmly into the top half of the First Division among the parish churches of England, along with Holy Trinity, Hull, and Boston, Lincs, with St. Wulfram at Grantham and St. Mary Magdalen at Newark, with Walpole St. Peter in Norfolk, with Long Melford and Mildenhall and the churches of the Golden Age along the coast of Suffolk.

At St. Mary Redcliffe it is quite certain that the transepts are not of the same date. One feature, not immediately obvious, clearly distinguishes the south transept from the rest of the church. From the interior one can see that its main vault is in fact quite considerably lower than those of the adjoining choir and nave or of the north transept opposite. Few visitors notice this, since the arcades of all four arms of the church are of equal dimensions. But from the outside of the church, and noticeable only from due east and to a less extent from the south, one can see that the south transept has a large space above the vault, with bare unpanelled walling east and west, and a small window to the south lighting the considerable space above the vault. But for the rest of the church the apex of each clerestory window reaches almost to roof level. Originally the south transept seems to have had a steeply pitched roof, until its walls were raised to conform to the subsequent parts of the church.

Two features of the exterior are important in creating an effect of unity. The first are the pierced parapets which create a strong horizontal effect

Skelton engraving of the transepts, from John Britton, 1813.

which counter-acts the vertical of the mullions of the windows and of the blank panelling used everywhere except on the south transept, and secondly the buttresses. In fact the flying buttresses themselves are not of the same design all round the church. Only those of the south transept are crocketed but all are enlivened by being pierced as they join the clerestory wall. Comparison may be made with the flying buttresses of the presbytery of Winchester Cathedral, work of somewhere near 1500.

Inside the church one detail emphasises the continuity between the south nave aisle and the lower parts of the south transept and is easily noticed: the wall above the bench and below the aisle windows is plain. Subsequently, in the choir, north transept and nave the same area is decorated with perpendicular panelling.

The inside of the south transept is also quite distinct from the latter parts of the church in that the wall above the main arcade is treated differently. There is a strong horizontal at the level of the apex of the arcade with pointed trefoils in each spandrel. This is reminiscent of similar motifs in a similar position in the choir of Ely Cathedral (begun 1332), following the collapse of the central tower. Another East Anglian feature is the ornamentation of the horizontals of the panelling above the arcade and below the window with machicolations.

The design of the clerestory windows is quite eccentric and personal, with a circuit of thirteen quatrefoils bordering the inner three lights. A border of quatrefoils around a window is also found in Bristol in the south aisle of St. Mark's, the Lord Mayor's Chapel. Another example is the south rose at Lincoln Minster but most extraordinary of all is the east window of the chancel of Mildenhall, Suffolk: an inscription on a brass, now lost, recorded that the donor was Richard de Wichforde, vicar from 1309-1344.

Bands of quatrefoils occur also in works connected with the Ramsey family of masons, as around the doorway into the great hall of Penshurst Place, Kent, and in the choir of Lichfield Cathedral as well as in the Perpendicular work at Gloucester Cathedral, at the foot of the choir gallery. This feature also occurred around the foot of the upper storey of William Ramsey's now destroyed cloister of old St. Paul's. Once again the connections of work at St. Mary Redcliffe are national, and with the most recent innovations as the style of English architecture was being transformed from Decorated with all its variety to the more sedate Perpendicular.

The great south window of the south transept is yet another surprise.

Vault of north transept. Photo: *Damian Gillie.*

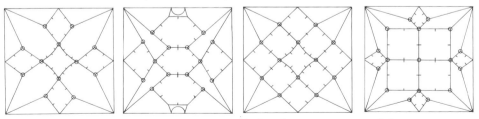

Vault designs: (left to right) *South transept east aisle.*
South choir aisle. North choir aisle. South porch.

There had been earlier great transept windows, for instance that in Hereford Cathedral north transept (c. 1255), but the south window here is more distinctively Bristolian in character.

Its ancestors are to be found in the new Lady Chapel and choir of St. Augustine's Abbey (Bristol Cathedral), for those windows too have the boldly traceried horizontal transoms which unify the design, leading the eye vertically and yet, by the intertwining of ogee curves, at the same time inter-locking the design into a unit. Similar developments were taking place in Tuscany, as in the choir of S. Croce in Florence and the nave of Siena Cathedral, the construction of which was interrupted by the Black Death: there seem to be links with Bristol. It is noticeable that the tracery of the great south transept window at Redcliffe is still essentially Decorated, that is to say, curvilinear in pattern. The window opposite, in the north transept, one might perhaps expect to have been given a more soberly and more sedate Perpendicular framework: but it was not. Only the glass is so different that the windows look unmatched.

What makes St. Mary Redcliffe so exceptional, and indeed beyond compare, is that it is vaulted throughout. The vault patterns vary greatly, and so does the quality of the carving of the roof bosses.

The vaults of the transept aisles are designed as distinct bays, as are those (to a different design again) of the high vault. The curved rib design of the south nave aisle was used again, but not developed, for the south transept aisles. Elsewhere round the church, the masons seem to have relished the chance to design variously complex patterns, not notably discordant one from the other. This process could be permitted since it does not disrupt the overall unity of the design of the church. Most visitors do not notice the changes in vault design.

The saddest feature of the south transept, and indeed of the north, is that Victorian seating arrangements suggest a north-south axis. But it seems certain that at least the eastern bays of the transepts were designed to provide separate chapels facing eastwards. Indeed, the focus towards the high altar was so strong that squints were cut through the corners between transepts and choir aisles; but now the floor has all been levelled and the sense of direction in these parts of the building absolutely disturbed. It is only when looking at the vaults and bosses that the orientation of what were once chapels in the eastern aisles of the transepts becomes obvious.

For those with good eyesight or binoculars the bosses are worth detailed inspection. The main ones of the high vault of the south transept represent the Three Persons of the Trinity, while those of the left hand chapel in the eastern aisle include the best set of religious bosses - including the Annunciation, Madonna and Child, the Resurrection and the Coronation of the Virgin.

It may be safely assumed that the form of the choir, four bays long, with a further bay to include the ambulatory, and of the Lady Chapel, initially only one bay in length, was decided upon at one time. The east end is not designed, like Worcester or Bristol Cathedral, with a 'high east end' with the vault height being maintained from the choir and over the ambulatory and Lady Chapel, but in the 'low east end' form as used earlier at Salisbury (1220) and also in a more complex form recently at Wells Cathedral.

A possible date for this work at Redcliffe is suggested by the survival of the Regulations for the Chantry of Eborard de Fraunceys 'in capella beate Mariae de la Redeclyve' in 1350; these are to be found copied into The Little Red Book of Bristol, f.80. Several subsequent mentions of the Lady Chapel in wills dating from later in the century seem to imply that work was still going on.

The most obvious feature of the choir is its height. As already noted, the Victorian masons discovered that the choir of the Early English church rose high: the evidence of the Early English vaulting is still visible in the nave, and this seems to have set the proportions for the later work. The remodelling of the church did not, on this evidence, involve the complete destruction of the earlier building, but quite clearly the time had been reached at which a final approved standard design had been accepted and remained unquestioned till the church reached completion.

There are one or two awkward joins which indicated the difficulties which the builders had to overcome on an uneven sloping site - the levels of mouldings at the junction between the Lady Chapel and north choir aisle do not quite coincide; but as a whole the sequence of parts is smoothly and harmoniously managed.

Everything at first glance looks very regular. Yet it soon becomes plain that campaign followed campaign in a slightly haphazard and spasmodic way. This is particularly evident from an attentive walk around the processional way, from the south choir aisle into the north choir aisle, and into the western bay of the Lady Chapel. The structural arches which form the openings of the windows are not all of one shape: three to the south, wide with hard angled tops; the eastern windows of the aisles two centred; the Lady Chapel different again.

Even more significant is the difference of vaulting between the south aisle of the choir and that of the balancing aisle to the north. The design of the rib-pattern is quite different and so is the character of the carving of the bosses, of which there are twenty four per bay on the south aisle but only sixteen on the north. Even more important is the different effect: the south aisle vaults are designed as a sequence of distinct bays, but the vault along the north aisle is conceived as a unit. This suggests that there was not only a different team of craftsmen, as indicated by the difference in the carving of the bosses, but also a different master-mason or architect in charge.

The east wall of the choir is dominated by its seven light window in the (restored) Perpendicular style, yet a trace of Decorated exuberance survives in the trefoils in the spandrels below it. For the rest of the church, however, one design is adhered to all the way down the choir and nave, and with but a minor variation in the north transept - an extra horizontal at the apex of the arcade, to balance the design used earlier in the south transept. The Perpendicular panelling which dominates the upper parts of the interior appears equally consistently around the exterior of the clerestory of the choir, nave and north transept. And all the windows of the clerestory round the same parts of the church are of a uniform pattern, with six lights for choir and nave, and five lights beneath the same sort of tracery in the north transept.

The vault of the choir is of a complex lierne pattern, with an arrangement of cusped diamonds and squares, and with the effect of a triple ridge rib. There are echoes of work in the choir vaults of Bristol and Wells Cathedrals and also reminiscences of the choir vault at Gloucester. In its settlement the vault has become a little eccentric, but this does not too seriously mar the general effect. The vault, as with those of so many of the Decorated period in the West of England, is meant, like that of the north choir aisle, to read as a unit. Though there are four bays of arcade with clusters of shafts rising to the vault, the main emphasis, achieved partly by the repetition of so many short verticals in the blank panelling and in the clerestory windows, is one of horizontal unity. The walls are capped by a single vault, continuous in impact from the east window to the great crossing arch.

The order in which operations were carried out in the nave is a puzzle. The west wall of the church is definitely characteristic, in detail, of mid fourteenth century Decorated, with nodding ogee arches, all cusped and crocketed. The effect is a little bizarre for the tracery of the great west window is straightforward, no-nonsense Perpendicular (and the glass in the over-familiar Victorian style of the Hardman studio). It seems then that the west wall of the nave was re-built in the Decorated period. This makes sense for the upper two storeys of the tower are clearly of this date. The design and detailing are consistent with an early fourteenth century date: in no respect can it be confused with the less profuse, more restrained panelled work so characteristic of Perpendicular at St. Mary Redcliffe.

That the spire was completed early in the fourteenth century is probable, if not absolutely certain. There is a record, slightly suspect, that the spire fell in 1445 or 1446, and there are many records of the truncated form which survived until the 1870s.

The design of the present spire is a little reminiscent of the fourteenth century spire of Salisbury Cathedral, or, in the impact of a tall spire rising from between four minor ones, comparison may be made with St. Mary's, the University Church at Oxford. A.K. Wickham, in his fine book *The Churches of Somerset* (new ed. 1965) noted that most of the eighteen spires on Somerset churches were built in the Decorated period.

The impact has been a good deal diminished in recent years by the building of tall office blocks. Through the latter middle ages the dominant features of the skyline of Bristol would have been the tall spires not only of St. Mary Redcliffe but also of other churches including those of St. John Baptist, now quite overwhelmed, and the great spire of the totally destroyed convent of the Carmelites.

Though built to a cathedral-like plan, in scale St. Mary Redcliffe is much smaller. It is 250 feet long overall; Exeter is 409 feet, Salisbury 473 feet. The transepts are 117 feet across, those of Salisbury 230 feet. Nonetheless the building, or remodelling, of a parish church on so lavish a scale must have been a considerable undertaking.

It seems likely, if not conclusive, that work had to be interrupted in the second half of the fourteenth century. Towards the end of the century the church most likely looked much the same as Cologne Cathedral did for three hundred years between the sixteenth and the nineteenth century, even perhaps with a crane still in position for the resumption of the work when times improved.

Though so much was going on in the church in the fourteenth century there is little evidence of a personal sort other than an effigy now resting in the western recess of the south nave aisle. It represents, almost life size, John Lavington who was recorded as vicar of Bedminster and Redcliffe in 1393; he died about 1411. The effigy was

Recess in south nave aisle, c.1330 with the effigy of John Lavington, c.1411.
Photo: Damian Gillie.

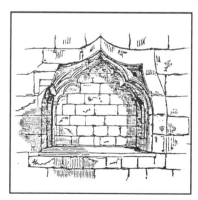

The tomb recess
before restoration
on discovery in 1852.

discovered in 1776 near the site of the western window of the Chapel of Holy Spirit, a chantry foundation near the south west corner of the church which was pulled down at this time.

The sculpture is rather flat and not very graceful; but it is in reasonable condition. The figure is shown with his tonsured head on a cushion, hands joined in prayer. His cassock has buttons on the cuff, with three more at the neck. He wears a belt, and slippers with straps at the instep. His name is inscribed at the foot of the slab.

There is a record in Britton (1813) of an effigy on a plain altar tomb to the memory of Eborard le French with an inscription that he died in 1350 having founded chantries at St. Mary Redcliffe and St. Nicholas, thrice been mayor of Bristol - in 1333, 1337 and 1339 - and twice represented Bristol in parliament. This tomb has since been entirely lost trace of - unless it is the effigy called Canynges' almoner, referred to in the next chapter.

It is not difficult to recapture the character of church life in St. Mary Redcliffe at the end of the fourteenth century. In 1380 there were probably twenty four chantry priests, and altars - not only the High Altar and one at the Lady Chapel but others - whose position is sometimes suggested by the carvings on the roof bosses - of St. Katharine, St. George, St. Nicholas (patron of sailors), St. Simon and Jude, St. Stephen, St. James, suggesting the pilgrimage to Santiago in N.W. Spain, and St. Blaise. A boss in the vault of the middle bay of the west aisle of the south transept shows a priest and a penitent. One of the great feasts of the year was the procession at Corpus Christi, but such events are suggested now only by Victorian paintings. Sermons were preached in the churchyard, presumably at the cross, ceremonial occasions with the Mayor of Bristol leading the worshippers.

By the end of the century Bristol was becoming very prosperous, with a population probably approaching ten thousand. Only London and York amongst English cities were larger. The prosperity of the port depended particularly on the export of cloth, the figures for which are indicative of the boom. In 1353-55, only 1,300 cloths were exported, in 1367 the total had risen to nearly 8,000 but after a recession in 1385-8, the total shot up to 43,000 in 1392-95. In this rich city rose St. Mary Redcliffe.

FURTHER READING

P. Zeigler: *The Black Death* (1970)

C.E. Boucher: 'The Black Death in Bristol', *Trans. Bristol & Glos. Arch. Soc. IX* (1938), pp 31-46

On architectural matters, again see

J. Bony: *The English Decorated Style* (1979), and also J. Harvey: *The Perpendicular Style, 1330-1485* (1978)

R.K. Morris: 'The Development of Later Gothic Mouldings in England c. 1250-1400', *Architectural History* 21 (1978), pp 18-57; and 22 (1979) pp 1-48

See too R.K. Morris' article on Thomas of Witney at Exeter, Winchester and Wells, in F. Kelly (ed.): 'Medieval Art and Architecture at Exeter Cathedral': *British Archaeological Conference Transactions for the year 1985* (1991), especially p. 73 for a firm attribution of work in St. Mary Redcliffe to William Joy.

For Bristol's overseas trade,

E.M. Carus-Wilson: *Medieval Merchant Venturers* (1954 and 1967)

The tomb recesses were illustrated at the time of their discovery in *Illustrated London News*, October 9 1852.

5

PERPENDICULAR:
THE CHURCH COMPLETED

As far as architecture is concerned the second half of the fourteenth century is largely a period of consolidation and of the completion of unfinished business... In the majority of towns and cities from Naples to the Alps it must have been impossible to walk more than a few hundred years before encountering an unfinished church or palace.

John White: *Art and Architecture in Italy 1250-1400* (1966)

Where experts differ it is necessary to make one's own attempt at reconstructing the history of events.

W.S. Bristowe: *The World of Spiders* (1958) chap.4: The Ancestry of Spiders

Different writers have offered different interpretations of the fragmentary evidence which survives to indicate the chronology of the later work in St. Mary Redcliffe.

One possibility is that by the end of the fourteenth century the church had reached a stage which simply required completion by later generations of patrons and masons.

The other possibility is that the church had been completed but that it was remodelled in the fifteenth century; such remodelling may have been prompted by damage caused when the spire fell in about 1445.

A personal interpretation of the evidence suggests a compromise between these extreme interpretations of the evidence: that the fall of the spire in mid-century necessitated some repairs and at the same time stimulated the completion, with some adaptations, of the original fourteenth century design. This work needs to be considered in the light of the involvement of the wealthy merchant family, the Canynges, in the history of the church and parish, and in the light of the first-hand documentation of the church by the contemporary antiquarian, William Worcestre. Finally, just before the Reformation, minor additions were made to the structure; the tombs and brasses of the period, and contemporary wills and other documents, indicate the significance of the church to the wealthiest and most influential citizens of Bristol.

Though for convenience such matters as details of design and building practice, the identity of architects and patrons, and the reports of a local antiquary are here dealt with one by one within the confines of a single chapter, it needs to be remembered that the period to be covered is about a century and a half - as if today we were looking back at the accession of Queen Victoria.

It may seem odd that work on the new St. Mary Redcliffe took so long, being started in the Decorated style and completed in Perpendicular. The work was perhaps not completed by 1480, or even later, having been begun in about 1320. But such a timescale was not unusual. At Oxford the college chapel at Merton was begun in c. 1290, but when the north transept was built in c. 1420 the south transept was altered to make it Perpendicular. A failure to complete long-term plans for rebuilding is the explanation for Bristol Cathedral having a Victorian nave and west front: Winchester Cathedral must have been a building site for centuries.

There are various ways of reconstructing a building's history. Historians put great trust in the written word, in documentary evidence, but for St. Mary Redcliffe such material is sparse, or worse

Exterior with south porch and south transept from the south east.
Photo: *Gordon Kelsey.*

still, suspect. In several cases - as scholars have recently pointed out - documents have been altered by much later and misleading additions. Some obscurities in the record must be attributed in particular to Thomas Chatterton whose activities will be considered in the next chapter.

Architectural historians are trained to read buildings, and are often, if the truth be told, more experienced in this than in reading ancient documents. The converse is true of most historians. Such details as mouldings, tracery patterns, vault designs and changes in the style of foliage carving, or details in the programme of roof-bosses and stained glass, often provide indicators to suggest a date for a particular section of a building. Alas, as far as St. Mary Redcliffe is concerned, such evidence is blurred because the Victorian restoration was carried out with such emphatic zeal, reducing variety to an overall conformity.

There is, as we have seen, good reason to believe that the south nave aisle with its adjoining porch, and subsequently the south transept, are in the Decorated style. Presumably, and almost certainly, the choir also had been completed before the Black Death in 1348. The choir would have been needed as soon as possible and completed earlier than the north transept. Although this is basically to the same design as its opposite transept, features - particularly in the panelled walls of the aisles and of the exterior of the clerestory, and in the tracery of the windows - indicate a date when Perpendicular was the dominant style. That is to say, the north transept could have been complete by the end of the fourteenth century.

Brakspear (1922) suggested that the fall of a presumed central tower related to structural problems in the north transept arising from irregularities in the foundations set on steeply sloping ground. It is abundantly clear from the outside that the present north side of the church is indeed supported on strong new work, including the vestry to the east and the undercroft of the north transept. In the 1930s part of these undercrofts was known, romantically, as Canynges' Kitchen. All this work is laid carefully and strongly; inside the church there is no sense at all of the unevenness of the site. Brakspear thought the undercroft under the north transept was originally intended to serve as a bone-hole to hold any burials disturbed during the remodelling of the rest of the church. If, as he suggested, these parts of the north transept were for a long time completed only to a low height, the effect must have been very odd - not unlike that even today at the incomplete chapel beyond the south transept of Glasgow Cathedral.

The Lady Chapel and north choir aisle, showing changes in levels.

The other major uncompleted work was the remodelling of the nave. The elevation of the nave walls is a continuation of the design used earlier in the choir, but the vaulting is different. The nave vaults, those over the crossing and under the tower may well date from as late as the second half or end of the fifteenth century. It would have been imperative for the crossing piers and arches to be supported by the adjoining bays in each direction, and as we have seen the west wall of the nave seems to be certainly of Decorated work; presumably the aisles would need to be completed before the upper parts of the church. The roof could have been on a for a long while, making the church watertight, before a stone vault needed to be completed.

That a general design had been agreed upon which later generations of masons respected would be consistent with medieval building practice. For example, when Bishop Grandisson succeeded the murdered Walter Stapledon at Exeter Cathedral, he found that great quantities of prepared stone and timber had already been obtained with which he could continue the work in the nave through the years 1342-1372. At the end of the first period of activity, in 1341-1342, the detailed records include a reference to the purchase of canvas to be used temporarily 'to close up the large gable at the (west) end of the church'. Ten years later, in 1350-51, payments for wattle and daub record the blocking up of window openings by unskilled labour, while skilled masons were paid to make sure that the stonework of the windows was left in proper order until glass and glaziers could be found. Similar records survive for the presbytery at Winchester. Meanwhile at Exeter, though the nave had a roof, it still lacked its stone vault. The Fabric Rolls for 1353 record the purchase of a net to keep pigeons out of the choir. Thus did even the richest in the land seek to complete schemes of rebuilding left incomplete in the years following the Black Death.

At parish church level, progress could often be equally spasmodic. Indeed one of the most characteristic features of most of our greatest parish churches is the haphazard way they grew after plans for complete reconstructions had, for various reasons, been abandoned. Two comparisons will suffice. The marvellous parish church at Cirencester has a complex history. Its Perpendicular nave dating from 1515 is, in the beauty of its slender piers and panelled walls and the general air of refined elegance, in several ways reminiscent of St. Mary Redcliffe. But Cirencester developed in a less coherent way than St. Mary Redcliffe: the nave and aisles, like the chancel and the various

View eastwards from north nave aisle across nave towards south transept.
Photo: *Damian Gillie.*

subsidiary chapels, all have timber roofs, apart from the St. Catherine's Chapel which was fitted with a fan vault in 1508, long after it had been built.

By contrast the intention when Steeple Ashton, in Wiltshire, was being rebuilt was that it should be vaulted throughout in stone, like St. Mary Redcliffe. There is a sense of disappointment when the visitor recognises that the nave vault, in design reminiscent of the choir vault at Redcliffe, is only of timber. Though many outstanding parish churches, both in Somerset and in East Anglia, have stupendously beautiful timber roofs, it is the stone vaults of St. Mary Redcliffe which give it a pre-eminence: not all our cathedrals have such a distinction.

As we consider the vaults, we move from the south choir aisle into the north to find that a new pattern has been used. Instead of fourteen bosses in each bay there are only twelve, and there is also a quite distinctive style of boss-carving. This new pattern, first used in the north choir aisle, was then adapted for use in the aisles of the north transept by the omission of the liernes which completed the outer of the two square patterns. Once again the style of the carving is different from that used earlier.

The sense of fun which a modern visitor to the church may enjoy in drawing little diagrams of these vault-patterns can be recognised in similar notebook drawings by the early thirteenth century French architect Villard de Honnecourt. That similar designs were made by the builders of St. Mary Redcliffe is indicated by the use of vault designs amongst the roof bosses of the eastern aisle of the north transept and of the north nave aisle. To see exactly the same sort of design built high above one's head is a thrilling experience. One boss has the design of a rose window rather reminiscent of the north rose of Notre Dame, Paris. Another echo of France is the presence of a maze on another boss: one of the happier events of the last few years has been the creation of a full- size maze in Bristol's Victoria Park to the same design.

We must now consider the detailing of the church, especially of the nave. A probably reliable indication for dating work at the north west of the crossing is provided in the aisle vault by bosses carved with the arms of Berkeley, Beauchamp, Stafford and Montacute. These may commemorate the betrothal of Lord Berkeley's daughter to Richard Beauchamp, son of the Earl of Warwick, and would indicate a date somewhere about 1392 (the contract) to 1397 (the marriage).

Both transepts, including the crossing piers - which for structural reasons must have been built with them - use the same pier form which has already been recognised within the south nave aisle. The major feature is a cluster of bold shafts in triplet form supporting a quite bold foliage capital below the springing of the vault. This pattern was used in turn for the north aisle of the nave.

Pier bases: north transept, north nave aisle and south transept.

Details of mouldings near ground level are always suspect since they can so easily be damaged and equally easily remodelled. It is, however, worth noting that in the south nave aisle the form of base moulding is quite simple. This can also be seen in the south transept but in a simplified form, perhaps pared down from the preceding one with the top ring missing. This form appears on the south face of the crossing piers; but it is noticeable that the southern sections are not bonded in with the rest of the piers.

On the other sides of the same piers it is easy to see that a more richly modelled base is used: it is this form which is retained for the rest of the church, including even the Lady Chapel.

A more significant change in design between the transepts and the remaining parts of the church is clearly visible in comparison between the forms of the main piers. Those of the transepts are diamond-shaped, with a hollow cut back into each face and triplet shafts added at each corner. But the piers of the choir and nave are square in plan, not diamonds; and although triplet shafts are still used to provide visual support to the mouldings of the main arcade and beneath the aisle vaults, on the front of the pier there is now a cluster of tiny shafts which rise, thin as pencils, uninterruptedly to the high vault. Instead of a leafy capital sprouting at the top of these so-slender shafts, there is only a minute ring.

The whole elevation along the east-west axis of the church is much more linear than that used for the transepts: the design can properly be

North transept. Watercolour drawing by T.L.S. Rowbotham, 1826.
Braikenridge Collection, City Art Gallery.

compared with those used for the royal chapels at Windsor or King's College, Cambridge.

Engravings made before the Victorian restoration show that in several places, particularly near ground level, there has been refacing and remodelling and this may well have obscured other details which would have illuminated the progress of the late medieval work. But if we remember how the choir of Wells Cathedral was remodelled, or most of Winchester, or Ripon or Worcester, it is evident that medieval masons were very experienced in carrying out most complex schemes, renovating an old building arch by arch, bay by bay.

The major feature which unifies the interior and the exterior of the church, the choir and the nave, the north transept and the adjoining north nave aisle, is the vertical panelling. George Pryce (1853) noted that during the Victorian restoration the north choir clerestory was found to have been Early English work resurfaced and remodelled in a Perpendicular style. Such refacing could have taken place spasmodically over many decades as money became available or when structural problems enforced repairs.

Similar panelling is a feature of the Sherborne choir, c. 1425, and at Great Malvern, c. 1440. The north transept clerestory windows, to east and west, are not in the capriciously extravagant forms used for their opposite numbers in the south transept but a 'regulation issue' Perpendicular like those used in the choir and nave. All these windows are to a consistent pattern of six lights, except next the crossing piers where there are but five.

The whole effect of a high vault depends greatly on the relationship to the clerestory windows below. The higher the point at which it springs from the wall at the sides of the glazed area, the lighter the effect. A vault which enfolds the clerestory windows, in the manner so sadly demonstrated by the nave vault at Tewkesbury, creates a very dark effect; but in the north transept of St. Mary Redcliffe the vault is so cleverly built that hardly anyone notices that the clerestory windows to east and west rise much higher than the top of the great north window. On the exterior the difference in height is a little more obvious; there is not a great space, as there is in the south transept, between the roof and the vault.

How may we interpret these facts? At the minimum, they seem to confirm that the upper parts of the choir, north transept and nave, were designed together, and that their design is a revised version of that created for the south transept before the Black Death. As a corollary to this, it is clear that the upper parts of the south transept were heightened to conform to the levels of the adjoining choir and nave.

The loveliest vault in St. Mary Redcliffe, and which impresses itself on the regular congregation as well as on the occasional visitor, is the nave vault. The complexity of its design defies analysis. Visually, with its multiplicity of liernes and cusps and bosses, it reads not as a succession of seven bays but as a single unit.

It is one of the most beautiful vaults even in the west country, an area in which the expertise of local masons was nowhere better displayed than in their vaulting. One significant comparison might be with the vaults of the north transept and crossing in Bristol Cathedral: these date from early in the sixteenth century. The assumption must be - for there are other earlier fine vaults in Bristol, as in the crypts of St. Nicholas and St. John Baptist - that Bristol masons had great expertise in building complex vaults, and that this expertise lasted over many generations. A particularly fine vault once existed in the neighbouring church of St. Thomas, of which only fragments, including roof bosses, now survive.

Though the vaults of St. Mary Redcliffe rise only to 54 feet the effect is heightened by the slenderness of the shafts which appear to support them and by the recurrent verticals of the panelling of the spandrels and of the clerestory mullions. Unlike so many contemporary parish churches, St. Mary Redcliffe does not have the open airiness of a preaching church. Comparisons with such churches as Terrington St. Clement in the Fens are therefore not very rewarding, though some writers have detected influences from St. Mary Redcliffe in the design of St. Nicholas, King's Lynn. Other writers have suggested connections with the churches of Coventry, or with St. Stephen at Norwich. But in its planning, its proportions and its vaulting, St. Mary Redcliffe remains unique.

Further evidence of possible use in dating the progress of the rebuilding of the church is contained in the collection of Bristol wills entered into the *Great Orphan Book* and edited in an abstracted form by T.P. Wadley in 1886.

In 1385, John Stanes or Stanys requested that he be buried in the new chapel and would leave 40 shillings if this were possible but only 20 if his burial was not permitted there. Was work still in progress? In the same year, Walter Derby made a bequest to the fabric of the chapel of Blessed Mary at Redcliffe. Nine years later, in 1394, Richard Calf made several bequests for architectural projects in various Bristol churches,

Vaults of the crossing and of the nave to the west.
Photo: *Damian Gillie.*

including work in St. Mary Redcliffe. In 1398, John Frenssh asked to be buried near the font, presumably in the nave.

That the reports of the spire of the church being hit by lightning in about 1445, causing much damage, are contradictory and suspect was first pointed out by George Pryce in 1861. In the records collated by the Climatic Research Unit at the University of East Anglia there is no confirmatory evidence, though in November and December 1446 there were great storms with thunder and strong winds.

The strong likelihood, considering the position of the spire, would be that if it was damaged in a storm it would fall, blown by a wind from the north west, across the church towards the south porch. If the wind had been from the south west the spire would have fallen on to the north porches which show no sign of damage. It is indeed on the south side of the church that there seem to be signs of alterations. The south porch, as already noticed, is in suspect condition with what appears to be a late vault interpolated to create a two-storied structure. In the nearby bay of the south nave aisle, one bay from the west where the bookstall now is, the bosses include a carving of a subject which became popular towards the end of the middle ages, the Arma Christi, which with other changes in the quality of the carving of the roof bosses may indicate repairs. As already noticed, the windows of the south nave aisle are Perpendicular in style rather than Decorated as might have been expected.

A later, fifteenth century date would also be preferable for the vault under the tower (though in 1958 Prof. Pevsner suggested it was early fourteenth century work). In this vault also there appears a boss with the Arma Christi, and another with the so-called Arma Virginis, a heart pierced by swords. The Arma Virginis appears also in the vault of the north nave aisle, two bays further east, and this seems certainly to be fifteenth century work.

The vault in the crossing must also date from late in the century: it is like that of the crossing of Salisbury Cathedral, dated 1479 from a record in the Fabric Roll, and like the slightly later one in Bristol Cathedral.

Most of the great churches of the south west have been provided with a vault at the crossing, even to the extent of closing off a magnificent lantern like that at Tewkesbury; other examples are at Wells, Bristol and Gloucester cathedrals. Guides often claim that such vaults were to counter strong draughts, but the main objective was surely aesthetic rather than practical. It will be recalled that at Exeter the cathedral has twin Romanesque towers in transeptal positions, and the fourteenth century vault can therefore run continuously from above the high altar all the way to the great west window, unifying the whole interior. Since St. Mary Redcliffe, for different reasons, does not now have a central crossing tower, the question as to whether the crossing should be vaulted presented only one possible decision. The effect of this decision was crucial, for the vault at the crossing unifies the entire church. The vista across both transepts would have been impaired by a lantern; the more significant directional urge from the nave towards the high altar in the choir is uninterrupted by any hiatus.

The unification of the church along the west-to-east axis is further reinforced by another element in the design, though one hardly notices it until looking up at the crossing vault. The crossing is rectangular in plan, not square, the arches towards the transepts being only a little wider than those of the main arcades of the choir and nave. This, and the overall panelling of the interior and the pencil-thin vaulting shafts, is one of the design features to reappear in a royal context, in Henry Janyn's design for St. George's Chapel at Windsor, begun in 1475, and subsequently in a work designed by Janyn's successor at Windsor, William Vertue's Bath Abbey begun in 1501.

Such a link can best be explained at a personal level, for when William Worcestre made his notes about St. Mary Redcliffe in 1480, the master mason to whom he spoke was a certain John Norton, free mason of Bristol. Perhaps the same John Norton is earlier recorded at Southampton, at Lambeth Palace, and in 1448-49 as Lathomus at the royal foundation, Eton College. And also we may presume that when Edward IV saw St. Mary Redcliffe he saw it with scaffolding on one part or other of the church.

The comparison with the Royal chapels is valid too on other grounds. Most, including King's College chapel at Cambridge, were built only very slowly, with many interruptions and ultimately with a number of modifications to their original designs. At Bath, it was left to the Victorians to fulfil the ambitions of the original patron and his architects and build a stone fan vault over the nave.

In our chronological survey of St. Mary Redcliffe we need now to consider its parishioners and patrons, especially as commemorated in their funeral monuments. In the easternmost bay of the north choir aisle, which was probably the site of an altar to St. Stephen, are the Mede tombs, dating from about 1475. In style these tombs are distinctive and provide firm evidence of what was fashionable at that date. Comparison may be made with the screenwork round the choir.

The tombs constitute a family memorial, with effigies of a prosperous merchant in generously cut tunic and cloak, all trimmed with fur, and his gracefully gowned wife. His feet rest on a dog of labrador size, hers on a pair of lap-dogs. These are in the western bay and nowadays are usually thought to be of Philip Mede (d. 1471) and his wife; in the eastern recess is an attractive small square brass to his son Richard (d. 1491) and his two wives. Although the left hand standing wife is in only plain dress, the husband and other wife are depicted kneeling before God wearing their prestigious heraldic surcoat and mantle. It is perhaps not greatly important that different authors have proposed different identities for the figures commemorated. In the present context, their significance is that here are commemorated members of a very wealthy family, who owned land in Bedminster, Failand and Wraxall and achieved distinction as mayors of Bristol and as the city's representative in parliament.

The architectural form of the pair of tombs is overwhelmingly rectangular. The fronts of the chests are ornamented with 16 + 16 panels of Perpendicular work like that used so extensively throughout the church; even more panelling of the same sort fills the backs of the recesses. But all this rectilinearity is relieved by the richly carved canopies where the crocketed arches are supported playfully by flying angels. The same conceit can be enjoyed in Long Ashton church where the tomb of Richard Choke, a judge who died in c. 1483, has a similar canopy, presumably the work of the same team of masons, though his is a more fanciful tomb-chest, and looks much livelier after recolouring. It is a pity that the only colour near the Mede tombs is Victorian.

There remains only one part of the structure of the church to consider: the extension of the Lady Chapel by a further bay. From inside the chapel it is easy to recognise where the original wall was taken down, and the original extent of the chapel is also indicated clearly by the position of the stair-turrets, now with restored Tudor tops. The new bay is set above a vaulted passage-way which, like the similar one at St. Gregory, Norwich, allowed processions to circulate within the perimeter of the churchyard. The tracery of the new work and the vaulting of the extra bay show the continuity of Redcliffe traditions in design. There is nothing which would offend a mason who had worked on the church in the 1350s. It is notable that medieval architects were not afraid to temper their originality so that the character of the work begun by earlier generations should be retained. The work of previous generations was respected, not abused: nowadays too frequently we are not so fortunate.

On the floor of the chapel, though probably not in its original position, is a splendid brass from 1439. Its learned inscription commemorates John Juyn (or Inyn), Recorder of Bristol and a Chief Justice of the King's Bench, who is depicted in his robes. In his will he left a gown and a cloak to his chaplain, and plate and vestments to the church. Nothing of these or many similar bequests affecting the religious life of the church survived the Reformation.

We are most fortunate to have the scholarly study by James Sherborne of the figure whose name is always connected with the latter phases of the medieval history of St. Mary Redcliffe, William Canynges (1402-1474), Mayor of Bristol and Dean of Westbury College, around whose name so many traditions have accumulated.

The earliest member of the family of whom records survive, in 1334 and 1341, was John Canynges I. It may be assumed that William Canynges I was his son, a joint Bailiff of Bristol in 1362, the first mayor of the newly-created city of Bristol in 1373, and subsequently four more times. Three times he represented Bristol in Parliament. His primary loyalty, as is indicated by the provisions of his will, proved on May 8th 1396, was to the church of the parish in which he lived, not to St. Mary Redcliffe as some early historians of the church believed, but to St. Thomas.

At some time after its original compilation a problematic phrase, perhaps representing a tradition going back to the seventeenth century, was interpolated into Ricart's *Calendar*, one of the major primary sources for the history of Bristol:

> William Canynges builded the bodye of Redcliffe church, from the cross Iles downewards. And so ye church was ffynished as it is nowe.

All the evidence would seem to support James Sherborne's statement that 'It is likely that he was a contributor to the work on Redcliffe church, but it may be unwise to attribute to him prime responsibility for the nave.'

We are not here concerned with every member of the Canynges family except insofar as their lives indicate the social and economic context of Redcliffe and the adjoining parish. William Canynges I's younger son, John, was sheriff in 1382, mayor in 1389 and 1392, and was the city's representative on one occasion in Parliament. He, too, lived in St. Thomas rather than Redcliffe, a clothier, foreign merchant and substantial property owner. His will was proved in March 1405, and indicates burial in St. Thomas.

Of John Canynges' sons, we are most interested in William Canynges II. His brother Thomas, it must be remembered, was very prosperous and served as Lord Mayor of London in 1456-57; so, too, did his step-brother, John Young, in 1466-67.

William Canynges II is recorded from as early as c. 1429-1435 as being a very important merchant and was to become an outstandingly great shipowner. William Worcestre, who loved lists, recorded the names of his ships and their tonnage - a huge total. For over eight years William Canynges employed over 800 men, a huge proportion of the working population of Bristol. The list of ships is still recorded in the church, a litany to the prosperity of this famous man:

> The Mary Canynges of 400 tons
> The Mary Redcliffe of 500 tons
> The Mary and John of 900 tons (described by James Sherborne
> as 'a giant')
> A galiot of 50 tons
> The Catherine of 140 tons
> The Marybat of 220 tons
> The Margaret of (?) Tenby of 200 tons
> The little Nicholas of 140 tons
> The Catherine of Boston of 220 tons
> Another, lost off Iceland, of about 160 tons*

William Canynges was Mayor of Bristol in 1441 and four times in subsequent years; three times he represented the city in Parliament. The site of his great house, which survived until just before the last war, has now been explored by archaeologists: it had a great hall, a four-storey tower, a private chapel, and was clearly a building of quality. One of its fine tiled floors was saved and is in the British Museum. It was in this much-to-be-lamented great house that William Canynges is supposed to have entertained Edward IV during his first visit to Bristol in September 1461 - an episode developed by Chatterton and celebrated in paintings by local artists in the Victorian period.

*Following William Worcestre, the reading Iceland is preferred to the lettering on the board, Ireland.

In 1467 William Canynges' wife Joan died, and for reasons now not fully understood, this most prosperous shipowner was quickly ordained by his friend Bishop Carpenter of Worcester. On March 12th he received the order of sub-deacon, of deacon on April 2nd, and of priest on April 16th 1468. He said his first mass on Whitsunday, May 17th 1468, in St. Mary Redcliffe. Long after his death, when much had been written and invented about his life and role in the history of the church, Canynges' name was invoked by those who in 1848 hoped to save the building. The Canynges Society is still active. It seems that once the Victorians had completed their restoration work, perhaps as late as 1895, a 'tradition' of commemorating Canynges' first mass was begun, and this commemoration is still maintained.

On June 3rd 1469 William Canynges became Dean of Westbury College, a foundation always closely linked to the see of Worcester. Only parts of the college survived the Civil War, but much of the work carried out in the fifteenth century, including the main gate and adjoining range, may be attributed to Canynges' presence there.

We are more concerned with William Canynges' connections with St. Mary Redcliffe. On May 10th 1466, he had endowed a chantry in the chapel of St. Catherine, and on October 13th 1467 another in the chapel of St. George: both chapels appear to have been in the south transept. On October 20th 1467 he gave £340 to the vicar and churchwardens, 'remembering the wishes of earlier benefactors, including his own forebears'; this money financed two chaplains, one of whom was called Canynges' priest.

William Canynges drew up his will on November 12th 1474, and died a week later, on November 19th 1474. In the Great Red Book of Bristol, f. 247, William Canynges is described as

> renovator and as it were in other respects founder and among others a very special benefactor of the church of Redcliffe.

James Sherborne has indicated that this passage continues and reads that he and others were said to have paid

> masons and workmen to repair, edify, cover and glaze the church at Redcliffe.

Since the subject is so important to all who visit or guide visitors to the church, not only should James Sherborne's pages be considered, but also the words of two earlier students of the records.

In 1950 Edith Williams wrote

> It can be argued that William Canynges's work on Redcliffe
> might be too well known to need repeating, but Wyrcestre
> was so fond of detail and obviously a great admirer of
> Canynges that it is not easy to believe that he would refrain
> from mentioning it, if much had been done.

George Pryce (1854) was more vehement:

> Laudatory, oft-repeated tales, have obtained among us, until
> their very repetition has invested them with the semblance of
> truth. Such relations may amuse the masses, but will fail to
> interest the thoughtful when investigation has stripped them
> of their time-honoured embellishments and exposed their
> fallacy to the gaze of the inquisitive.

There is in fact hardly any visual evidence in the church itself, apart
from the Canynges tomb and the famous effigies, to link William
Canynges and the progress of the construction of the building. A
merchant's mark which appears on a piece of ancient glass re-set in one
of the small windows of the vestry was also found, during restoration
work, on one of the stones of the nave vault; and when Professor
Tristram cleaned and recoloured the tomb in the south transept, he
recorded (and restored) the same merchant's mark on the front
panelling of the tomb chest. The other repainted device, with the three
negro heads on a shield, is also attributed to William Canynges.

The monument is in the prime position in the south transept at the
foot of the great south window, partly blocking it. The great canopy
which emphasises the importance of the tomb is supported on four
octagonal uprights with castellated tops, as if for gigantic candles. The
broad horizontal, topped with foliate cresting, has a repainted
inscription asking for prayers; this is supported by a rather heavy four-
centred arch, with cusped sub-arches terminating in angels. The tomb
chest is panelled in unexciting Perpendicular fashion. Another tomb in
Bristol of the same sort, that of Bishop Miles Salley (c. 1516) in St.
Mark's, the Lord Mayor's Chapel, is more refined in its detail.

William Canynges and his wife Joan are depicted at approximately
life-size. Both figures are of freestone, and like the whole monument
have been recoloured. Joan is shown as if in prayer, wearing a veil, her

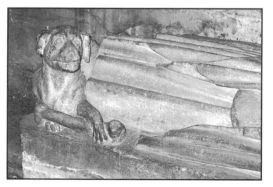

Canynges memorials:
1. Alabaster effigy of William Canynges, died 1474, as a priest, south transept.
Photo: Damian Gillie.
2. William Canynges with wife, south transept.
3. Gravestone of Canynges' cook.

4. Dog and bone: at foot of effigy reputed to be that of Canynges' almoner, west aisle of south transept.

head on a cushion supported by angels. She wears six rings, and has a pretty buckled belt at the waist of her flowing gown. At her feet are two dogs (one beheaded) with collars.

Her husband is shown as being rather taller, bald and clean shaven. Once more there are two angels at the head, but only one dog. The figure is dressed in the manner traditional for a rich fifteenth century businessman, with his long-sleeved gown trimmed with fur; the extravagant long pipe of his turban stretches from his shoulders almost to his ankles.

Both effigies have been trimmed to squeeze them on to the top of the tomb chest: this should alert us to suspect the present condition both of the monument and of the effigies. It is known that in the nineteenth century the effigies were removed from the south transept and for a while placed in the great tomb recesses in the south nave aisle. It was at this time that the eastern end-stop of the eastern recess was carved in the form of a negro's head: the bearded, bald man's head in the complementary position to the west is quite clearly Victorian.

There is a tradition, found for example in Dallaway (1834), that the alabaster effigy of a priest now in the south transept, always taken to be a memorial to William Canynges, was transferred from Westbury College after its destruction during the Civil War. There is however a probability that it had been moved about a century earlier than this, at the Dissolution of the College in 1544. The effigy is impressive not only for its size but for its quality. A priest is shown in choir habit, his cushion supported by angels. At the feet is a dramatic feature, a reclining saracen: it is not unlikely that the idea for this, and for the use of a saracen's head as a badge or device, derived from Spain where similar images are to be found in many cathedrals and churches, symbolising the reconquest of that country from the Moors.

The face of the alabaster effigy of the priest has been accepted by many writers and artists as a portrait of William Canynges. Alabaster is a very soft, fine grained stone which proves very adaptable to the carver, whether he wishes to counterfeit the textures of Yorkist armour or ladies' costumes, or the details of hairstyles and faces. How effective alabaster if for facial features can be seen by making comparison with the rather macabre effect of the painted freestone faces on the neighbouring monument.

There is, especially among specialist students of English medieval tomb sculpture, a very strong reluctance to accept that effigies in Gothic England were intended to display portrait-likenesses: the prime aim was to represent status. Even the alabaster image of a priest usually accepted as memorialising William Canynges and which has an apparently individualised face seems suspect as a portrait, for similar facial features were also used for the alabaster effigy of a judge, Sir Richard Newton, at Yatton, Somerset. The judge died in 1449 but the tomb was probably erected at the death of his second wife, who is also commemorated, in 1475. Whether the effigy of the priest and of the judge were carved near the quarries around Tutbury and Chellaston - or more probably in a London workshop - is not known. Certainly these alabaster effigies were imports, not local products carved from local materials. The carver is unlikely to have known either of the deceased.

Above the effigy of the priest is a wooden panel with a long and attractive inscription including the list of William Canynges' ships: this is apparently derived from William Worcestre's notes, and may be the work of a famous Elizabethan writer of epitaphs, the aptly-named Thomas Churchyard.

North of the Canynges tomb is another effigy, a very rough and vigorous crude piece of carving of a merchant. Like Canynges on the adjoining tomb he rests his head on his extravagant hat or turban; his tunic is generously cut with many deep-cut folds of cloth, and he has a full cloak, doubtless of the best quality material. His feet in pointed shoes rest on a memorable mongrel hound with a large bone. Romantics have identified the figure as being Canynges' secretary or almoner. Clearly he was a person of some local importance, and perhaps of particular significance in the history of the church, especially if this was the effigy which Barrett and others recorded near the crossing rather than cramped up against the wall.

On the floor not far from the great monument to William Canynges and his wife are two slabs which relate to this man's household. One slab is engraved with a large cross and has around its edge a long inscription to John Blecker and to Richard Coke and his wife Tibota; John Blecker is described as 'pandoxator' and is thus supposed to have been brewer to William Canynges. Nearby, another slab is engraved with bold representations of a kitchen knife, a pierced colander and an inscription:

Hic jacet Willm Coke quondam servitii Willmi Canynges mercatore ville Bristole an aie propitietur Deus. Amen.

Great men have their places in our history books, but their cooks and secretaries do not often have memorials even beneath the pews of our churches and cathedrals. The recent opening up of this part of the church is a great improvement.

Even more revealing than any of these memorials and more readable than the wills of those which they commemorate are the muddled notes made by the hero of all Bristol antiquarians, William Worcestre.

William Worcestre was born in Bristol in 1415, the son of William Worcestre, a burgess, and Elizabeth Botoner whose surname, a distinguished one in Bristol at that time, he sometimes used. After an education at Oxford University he served as secretary to Sir John Fastolf of Caister Castle, near Great Yarmouth. In this capacity William Worcestre travelled extensively not only throughout England but also into Normandy. He lived at various times at Castle Combe, in London and Cambridge, but towards the end of his life near St. James church, Pockthorpe, just to the north of Norwich Cathedral. He died in c. 1480-83. He worked in the circle of the Paston family whose letters provide so vivid an impression of the stresses of life in dangerous fifteenth century England. Several of the *Paston Letters* refer to William Worcestre's dispute with that family concerning the provisions of Sir John Fastolf's will.

The most fascinating of all William Worcestre's books and letters to have survived is material now included in ms. 210 in the library of Corpus Christi College, Cambridge. This is his notebook, 312 pages of various sorts of paper, about 28 x 11 cm., on which are written rough notes made in 1478, 1479 and 1480, on journeys made from Norwich even as far as St. Michael's Mount. The lists and notes he made, including many diverse records of such curiosities as stalactites in Wookey Hole and puffins in the Scilly Isles, were doubtless to be the basis of an archaeological and antiquarian survey of the whole country. What particularly concerns us amongst all this material, somewhat chaotically arranged and written, with gaps to be filled in later, with repetitions and several inconsistencies, are the records William Worcestre made of his native city Bristol, especially as they relate to the church of St. Mary Redcliffe and to the Canynges family. As he paced out the floor measurements of the churches he visited, he talked to the architects (if we may use that word) and masons:

Memorandum - to ask Robert Everard of Norwich this

question: How many inches does the spire of Trinity Church (i.e. the cathedral) batter in six feet? Freemasons: Benedict Crosse; John Norton, freemasons of Bristol.

Was there a discussion of Robert Everard's new spire, rebuilt after a thunderstorm had destroyed its predecessor in 1463 and damaged so much of the cathedral? Certainly William Worcestre was interested in the details of the mason's craft, for he noted down all the correct names of the mouldings of the south porch of St. Stephen's from Benedict Crosse, and for the west door of St. Mary Redcliffe from John Norton. In another passage William Worcestre describes the outer north porch, and there are measurements and lists of how many windows or mouldings. It is a fascinating but infuriating miscellany, giving a vivid impression of the man and his interests.

William Worcestre's knowledge of St. Mary Redcliffe was not that of a passing tourist. He was Bristol-born, and it is his sister Joan who is commemorated, with her husband John Jay, on the brass on the south side of the choir just before the high altar. The images of husband and wife in their best clothes, with their six sons and eight daughters, are for the parish of St. Mary Redcliffe the equivalent of the elegant donor-groups in Early Netherlandish altar-pieces by such artists as Hans Memlinc. The brass is interesting too for its architectural quality, for the figures are shown under a most elegant vaulted canopy ornamented with pinnacles, and with shields depicting what is probably a fuller's club and Jay's merchant's mark.

Jay was an important figure in the port of Bristol, his most famous exploit being to send two ships in 1480 to search across the Atlantic for the Isle of Brazil.

The other brass before the high altar is equally interesting. It shows a lawyer and his wife, with the inscription:

> Here lies the body of that venerable man John Brook, sergeant-at-law of that most illustrious prince of happy memory, Henry VII, and Justice of Assize for the same king in western parts of England, and Chief Steward of the honourable house and monastery of the Blessed Mary of Glastonbury, in the county of Somerset, which John died on the 25th day of the month of December, in the year of our Lord 1522. And near him rests Joanna his wife, one of the daughters and heirs of Richard Amerike, on whose souls may

Brass commemorating John Jay, his wife Joan and fourteen children, c.1480, choir. Photo: Gordon Kelsey.

God have mercy. Amen

The family name 'Amerike', in conjunction with the exploits of Bristol merchants as explorers and venturers across the Atlantic, stimulated another Redcliffe tradition: an explanation for the origin of the name America. The other interesting footnote, in Davis (1899), is that John Brook's father lived in Canynges' great house in Redcliffe Street.

Another Redcliffe muddle has confused a whale bone now in the tower, and perhaps brought back by Cabot, with the legend of Guy of Warwick slaying the Dun Cow. Such confusions grow in the re-telling.

What the interior of St. Mary Redcliffe looked like just before the storm of the Reformation burst is difficult to visualise. The chantries were suppressed, to the benefit of the king and his commissioners in 1547-48. At this time 33 chantry priests in Bristol had to face redundancy. Most of the surviving evidence is documentary. The majority of visitors to St. Mary Redcliffe have no idea of the richness of the written records which document the late medieval history of the church and its people; yet when selected items are brought out for display and properly explained they always attract rapt attention.

The several wills made by Bristol citizens indicate that a church such as St. Mary Redcliffe would have been adorned with many tiny but valuable, richly worked items - sacred vessels, vestments adorned with jewels, shrines, lights, statues, manuscripts with precious covers. The church would have been busy with all the appropriate Masses and Hours of the Dead as required by the terms of wills and regulated by the practices of the Sarum Rite. All the administrative work involved in running a busy church - paying chaplains, paying for anniversary obligations, administering the endowments which financed the running of the chantries - involved a great deal of paperwork.

For a chantry founded for Eborard le French in 1350 there survive records of a missal, a gilded chalice with a silver spoon, a corporal with a burse, three pairs of vestments, three altar towels, a hand towel and a pair of cruets. Each item in a 'chapel' or set such as this needed to be listed and valued conscientiously in an inventory. Something of the way of life for a chaplain, Robert Fychett of the same chantry, is indicated by the provisions of his will, made in 1510. He lived, we may deduce, in a place with a little chamber with hangings and his own mazer; a bed or cupboard is mentioned; he bequeathed three pairs of sheets and a coverlet to named beneficiaries, but left another sheet and a half to be used as altar-linen for the chantry which he served in St. Mary Redcliffe. He also bequeathed his clothes - one set consisting of a short gown, jacket, doublet and hose, and to others he left a silk gown, a furred jacket, a violet gown with a hood, a best surplice (so presumably he had another, not so good); and also bow and arrows. The income for Eborard le French's chantries, two in St. Nicholas and two in St. Mary Redcliffe, totalled just under £25 per annum: the two chantry priests in St. Mary Redcliffe were each paid £6 per annum.

The records for the Mede chantry indicate the same sort of financial arrangements as do those of the two chantries founded by William Canynges. The records of the chantries of William Canynges are indeed comprehensive and were published by a former archivist of St. Mary Redcliffe, Edith Williams. It is impossible and unnecessary to repeat all that material here. But two records may be selected for special attention.

The first is the full and justly famous record of the Easter Sepulchre which William Canynges gave to the church in 1474. This was a structure of timber and cloth, with images of sleeping soldiers, eight angels 'well peynted', and images of God the Father and God the Holy Ghost. This description was accepted by Horace Walpole (whom we shall encounter again in a Chatterton context) for inclusion in his *Anecdotes*, one of the first of English histories of art.

The second document is William Canynges' long and detailed will, of November 12th 1474. He wished to be buried 'in the place which he had constructed and made on the south side of the church, by the altar of St. Katherine where the body of his late wife Joan was buried.' He expressly detailed the lighting of candles, and left the church two lectionaries. People connected with the church are singled out, including Nicholas Pittes the vicar, two chaplains at the chantries of St. Catherine and St. George, three clerks, three procurators, and the keeper of the box for oblations at the north door of the church. Besides family and other beneficiaries he also remembered his six servants. But is should be noted that the majority of his bequests were to the church and college at Westbury on Trym, not to St. Mary Redcliffe.

Even more vivid than such fragile documents, written perhaps in a forgotten language and in handwriting which can be deciphered only through a magnifying glass, are the profusion of carvings on the roof bosses and the paintings in the beautiful fragments of stained glass. Studying these, perhaps through binoculars, can fill the eye and mind with the colour and imagery of the later middle ages and give even better than the architecture an idea of the character and quality of pre-Reformation devotion.

The wounds of Christ roof boss, tower vault. Photo: *Nora Hardwick.*

In the nave vault a number of bosses deserve especial notice. In the westernmost bay can be seen Christ on a rainbow, representing the Last Judgement, and also the Virgin and Child, patroness of the church. One bay further to the east is a representation of the symbols of the Four Evangelists, and of the Trinity. There is not, however, a consistent programme for the bosses as there is, for example, in the nave of Tewkesbury or Norwich. Nevertheless, what now appear to be random positions for particular carvings , as with the female saint near the door in the north nave aisle, may be an indication of the site of a medieval altar or chapel.

The entire loss of all original colour means that it is now impossible to interpret the significance of several bosses which show angels bearing smooth shields, but in the south nave aisle and in the vault under the tower are carved bosses showing a heart pierced by swords and symbols of the Passion. These reflect late medieval devotions to the Sorrows of the Virgin and the Wounds of Christ - the sort of devotions to which the severest of Reformers objected violently.

The glass now collected together in the windows of the tower is even more important for a proper understanding of what St. Mary Redcliffe looked like on the eve of Reformation. It is very beautiful and deserves careful scrutiny.

The most legible of the surviving glass is that now in the west window of the tower. In total there are nine major figure-fragments for which parallels are to be found in windows in Somerset churches, particularly at Langport and Trull. Whether all these windows were made in Bristol is not known, though there seems to have been a workshop in the area. The figures are a bishop in mass vestments; a Madonna and Child, perhaps the figures recorded by Pryce in 1861 as being in the north transept; an archbishop, perhaps St. Thomas Becket, with his head missing; St. Lawrence with his grid-iron; St. Michael; St. Matthias, with a phrase from the Apostles' Creed usually attributed to St. Matthew; St. John the Baptist; a woman and child, perhaps St. Elizabeth; the lower parts of a Crucifix from a representation of the Trinity.

The many fragments of glass collected together in the north window are well worth studying individually, for they provide evidence to supplement that of the fragments in the west window. There are heads probably of four more Apostles, so we may assume that there was once a set of Twelve Apostles as survive from a little later at Fairford. The five heads of female saints could well have come from another group; such large figures may have filled the main lights of windows either in the clerestory or in the aisles.

St. Michael is a figure usually connected, as at Fairford, with the Last Judgement, but all these major figures are typical of late medieval devotion, particularly to the Passion and to the Virgin.

Much smaller, and usually in the form of roundels which might have fitted into the narrow spaces of tracery, are many fascinating and attractive pieces. Some pieces seem to belong to sets: a monk and a head of St. Peter the Martyr seem to go together, as do two kings, and a pope and a bishop, and a group of evangelists' symbols. The most amusing are the roundels with grotesques: a dog with a man's head is very fine, and so is a winged deer. Similar roundels of the same character can be seen in the Erpingham window at Norwich Cathedral, in York Minster and in the Burrell Collection.

Other parts of sets are non-figurative, including especially decorative knots. But not the least significant of the various fragments in the north window of the tower are the very many pieces of Royal badges and cognisances, especially Yorkist suns, roses, suns in glory, all of them relevant to Edward IV whom William Canynges as mayor entertained in 1461. Probably these badges fitted small tracery lights - similar ones still survive in the transom of the west window of the south transept of the cathedral - rather than as backgrounds to portraits as in the Yorkist family series at Canterbury or Great Malvern.

There are also fragments of inscriptions, and amongst the roundels ones with letters which spell out the dedication of the church:

M.A.R.Y.

FURTHER READING

For building records, see for example H.E. Bishop and E.K. Prideaux: *The Building of the Cathedral Church of St. Peter at Exeter* (Exeter, 1922)

J. Harvey: *William Worcestre: Itineraries* (1969)

J. Dallaway: *Antiquities of Bristow in the Middle Centuries; including the Topography of William Worcestre, and the Life of William Canynges* (Bristol, 1834)

J. Sherborne: *William Canynges, 1402-1474* (Bristol Branch of the Historical Association, 1985)

Besides I.M. Roper and A.C. Fryer, see also

A. Gardner: *Alabaster Tombs of the Pre Reformation Period in England* (1940)

C.T. Davis: *The Monumental Brasses of Gloucestershire* (1899, reprinted 1969). The two brasses rescued from Temple Church are on the wall of the south choir aisle.

For John Inyn, and Inyn's Court, see *Malago*, number 12.

C.J.P. Cave: *Roof Bosses in Medieval Churches* (1948)

C. Woodforde: *Stained Glass in Somerset, 1250-1830* (1946, reprinted 1970); a full study of all the glass in the church is in preparation.

D.B. Quinn: *England and the Discovery of America, 1481-1620* (1974)

A.E. Hudd: 'Richard Ameryk and the name America' in H.P.R. Finberg: *Gloucestershire Studies* (1957), pp 323-29.

I. Wilson: *The Columbus Myth: Did Men of Bristol Reach America before Columbus?* (1991)

R.W. Pfaff: *New Liturgical Feasts in Later Medieval England* (1970), esp. chap. V.

6

AFTER THE REFORMATION:
HOGARTH AND CHATTERTON

'Historians, you think,' said Miss Tilney, 'are not happy in their flights of fancy. They display imagination without raising interest. I am fond of history - and am very well contented to take the false with the true. In the principal facts they have sources of intelligence in former histories and records, which may be as much depended on, I conclude, as anything that does not actually pass under one's observation; and as for the little embellishments you speak of, they are embellishments, and I like them as such.'

Jane Austen: *Northanger Abbey*
(1798) chap. XIV

St. Mary Redcliffe, as we have seen, was not the product of one age; its building was the work of many generations of patrons, architects and craftsmen working in a variety of styles. Though in the medieval period many of the towns and cities of England were provided with equally large parish churches - Grantham, for example, or Abingdon, Melton Mowbray or Boston, King's Lynn or Great Yarmouth, Coventry and many more - few of these churches were so beautifully integrated. The church is narrow and tall and vaulted, which gives it its own character quite distinct from other such great churches as Beverley or Hull or Nottingham. It has its own bay-rhythm with one huge clerestory window to each bay of arcade quite unlike the two-in-a-bay rhythm of so many great parish churches in East Anglia. But like most of these great churches throughout the length of England, St. Mary Redcliffe nowadays bears the evident mark of modern, post-reformation rather than medieval taste.

In the following chapters two topics will prove to be of major importance: the maintenance of the structure of the building, and the provision of the new furnishings needed by each succeeding generation to replace those adornments to the routine of worship which were so thoroughly destroyed as the Reformation ran its course.

Changes took place spasmodically, it needs to be remembered, not all at once. More than one generation of worshippers had to live through tempestuous periods of controversy.

In the reign of Edward VI, in 1547, the chantries were dissolved, including the two founded by William Canynges. The Crown confiscated all the plate, the lamps, all the vestments and the service books. Nothing, it seems, survived. In the same year the orgy of destruction, which had been rumbling on since 1538-39, continued in another outburst of iconoclasm when zealots working on the authority of Royal Injunctions broke all the 'superstitious images' whether carved in wood or stone, modelled in metal, whether painted on panels as altarpieces or in glass in the windows or on vellum in the books. The Churchwardens' Accounts for St. Mary Redcliffe begin in 1548. Two years later they record the obliteration of any paintings which had survived: the whole church was entirely repainted at the cost of £7. 3s. 4d. - 'a huge sum'. Altars were removed and the whole balance of the interior transformed for ever by the destruction of the rood screen at the high altar, an undertaking which cost £1. 3s. 0d. In 1552 the second, more Protestant version of the Book of Common Prayer was introduced only three years after the first new English order of service. In 1552-53

Interior in 1808, with the Hogarth triptych in situ.
Drawing by E. Bird, engraved by W. Angus.

payments had to be made 'for making of the Inventories unto the Commissioners for the plate and ornaments that was in the church for the Kynge'.

For a while, under Mary, the old Faith was restored and the parish churches of Bristol had to try to restore the old forms of worship, paying for replacements for the old books and vestments and holy vessels. But on November 17th 1558 it is recorded that the bell-ringers were paid 2s. 2d. 'for to ryng at the proclomacion of the quene's grace Elizabeth that now ys'. From this period also can be traced the first names of organists. Thus two great Redcliffe, Church of England, traditions go back this far continuously. In 1560 the last relics of Popery, the stone altars, were destroyed at the cost of 3s. 4d. As Dr. Bettey has written

> So thorough was the destruction of medieval furnishings and decoration in the Bristol churches during the sixteenth century that only a little now survives to enable the visitor to appreciate the former splendour.

One significant memorial of the new order of things is the Breeches Bible on display in the north choir aisle, a book printed in Geneva and a potent symbol of the new Protestant faith which had sprung to life in Germany and Switzerland as well as in England.

As the Reformation ran its dreadful course, Bristol had its martyrs. Two weavers, both men of Redcliffe, John Barney and his son had been amongst those prosecuted for heresy in 1498-1501. Among the six Bristolians martyred for their faith in the Marian period was Richard Sharpe of Redcliffe who died on May 7th 1537: his case is well documented.

Most guide books devoted to St. Mary Redcliffe or to the whole city of Bristol have somewhere or other included the traditional phrase 'one of the most famous, absolute, fairest and goodliest parish churches in the realm of England'. Many writers have been so bold as to omit the opening words, 'one of...' which further advances the claim, though not so far as Canon Cartwright in his 1963 Guide who went so far as to state that 'St. Mary Redcliffe is accepted almost universally as the finest example of Gothic architecture in England'. But Miss Edith Williams, perhaps the best qualified historian ever to write about the church, pointed out in her 1950 book that the famous phrase has not yet been traced in any contemporary record of the visit of Queen Elizabeth I to

Bristol in 1574. In the local records of that event only recently published there is indeed no reference to the Queen being a visitor to St. Mary Redcliffe, though she is recorded as leaving the city through Temple Meads. All the other proceedings which celebrated the royal visit are by contrast recorded in great detail, albeit rather impersonally.

Queen Elizabeth I is however still represented twice in the church. The first survival is the charter of the free grammar and writing school. In the great opening initial is to be seen a version of the standard early image of the Queen, enthroned in full coronation robes with crown, orb and sceptre. Such images of this queen or of her father are not uncommon and can be seen in several churches and country houses in the area, but what makes such mass-produced icons so intimate is to see them on an individual charter for a specific locality.

The school used to be in the Lady Chapel until its restoration for ecclesiastical use in 1854. In it stood the spectacular wooden statue of Queen Elizabeth now kept under the tower. It is life-size, of wood and painted brightly like a ship's figurehead.

Claims have been made that it is of sixteenth or seventeenth century date.

Owing to the loss of all the medieval woodwork, the finest piece of any great note now in the church is the Elizabethan great chest kept now in the Lady Chapel. It bears the date 1593 and the name of the church, St. Mary Redcliffe, which allowed it to be identified when it turned up in Bath in 1881 and recovered for the church. The ends of the chest are carved, and the front with the symbols of Faith, Hope and Charity, all within arcades. The main inscription is 'Commune Ye One With Another'. As a work of art it can hardly be called symbolic of the new spirit of the renaissance: it is appealingly provincial in quality.

Neither in the quantity nor in the quality of its art did the Renaissance make much impact in Bristol: its most lasting effect was in new and long-lasting changes in education.

Though Bristol and the west country as a whole were greatly disturbed by the Civil War, the seventeenth century seems to have been the quietest in the history of the church and its fabric. The major influence was the Laudian revival of church ceremonial and imagery, a movement which depended on the revival, or perhaps even survival, of Gothic traditions.

By far the most attractive seventeenth century feature in St. Mary Redcliffe is the brazen eagle lectern which stands shining at the crossing. Such lecterns had been very popular in fifteenth century

The eagle lectern, presented 1638. Photo: *Gordon Kelsey.*

Europe, having been exported from their place of manufacture in the southern Low Countries to Italy and Spain as well as England. A very fine example, originally for St. Nicholas' church, is now kept in St. Stephen's.

The Redcliffe lectern is supported on three amusing little lions. On the globe on which the eagle stands is an informative inscription:

THIS IS THE FREE GIFT OF JAMES WATHEN SENIOR
OF THIS PARISH PINN MAKER ANNO DMNI 1638.

This inscription indicates that the donor was in the metal trade, but it does not imply that the donor had made it nor that it was made locally, and it is probable that the reverse is true for two other lecterns of similar design survive in Laudian Oxford, in Magdalen College chapel, dated 1633, and in Exeter College chapel, dated 1637. The former is documented in the college records as having been brought from London. The one element of the design of this group of lecterns which is characteristically Baroque is the form of the baluster which bulges like a pear: the medieval lectern in St. Stephen's has a shaft which is angular with polygonal elements entirely in keeping in a Perpendicular church.

Brazen eagle lecterns continued to be made for other Bristol churches throughout the century: St. James has one of c. 1690, but the one given to the cathedral in 1683 was sold to St. Mary-le-Port in 1802 and now survives only fragmentarily in the crypt of St. John Baptist.

The brass candlesticks on the high altar are also of seventeenth century date with bulging curves; even more beautiful is the early seventeenth century chandelier in the Lady Chapel - subsequently, it seems, inscribed with the date 1650. Chandeliers happily are used to light the whole church, although now with electric light.

As in most of the churches in Bristol, though some were sadly lost in the last war, St. Mary Redcliffe has a fine carved, and recently recoloured, achievement of the Royal Arms of the restored Charles II. Another example of the same reign is in St. Stephen's. It is a puzzle that the carvers could cope so well with the heraldic lion and unicorn and relish the curves of the billowing mantling and then prove so inept with the frames. As in the arms of Charles I in the neighbouring church of St. Thomas, the framework has classical elements including caryatids or herms which are embarrassingly weak. It is as if local, provincial craftsmen still had little confidence or personal understanding of this new-fangled style.

The seventeenth century memorials in St. Mary Redcliffe are equally hesitant and not of any artistic consequence: there are better and much grander examples in most of the other churches of the city. The most moving, though artistically negligible, is a small plain tablet in the outer bay of the eastern aisle of the south transept which records the effect of the great plague on one Redcliffe family:

> HERE LYETH THE BODY OF MARY YE
> WIFE OF WILLIAM PREWETT OF THIS
> PSH GENT WHO DECEASED THE
> 6th DAY OF JULY ANNO DOM 1645
>
> ALSO THE BODIES OF WILLIAM JOHN
> AND MARY PREWETT THEIRE CHILDREN
> WHO ALL DYED IN IUNE 1645

Opposite, on the west wall of the same transept, are two more seventeenth century tablets, c. 1675, which are slightly more ambitious in design. But like the frame for the Royal Arms, they are of very poor quality artistically even on a parochial, let alone an international, scale.

Yet one monument of the period is historically of international significance, that to Admiral Sir William Penn who died in 1670. Originally this, too, was in the south transept near his grave but is now set, too high, at the west of the nave. Artistically it is nothing spectacular, with little cannons on the top of a bulging entablature. Fixed to the wall above are his arms and armour arranged like a trophy and higher still the admiral's personal streamers which he had flown at the masthead in the Second Dutch War. The square colour, once red, is his Cromwellian flag.

Of Sir William Penn we know a great deal, not only from major naval sources. More intimately we can see a portrait of him by Lely, and meet him frequently in the pages of Pepys' *Diary*. Not all the entries are complimentary but they capture the man marvellously and are worth searching out and reading as a group. Across the centuries we can recognise an individual.

> 25 June 1667. Up, and with Sir W. Pen in his new chariot, which indeed is plain, but pretty and more fashionable than any coach he hath, and yet do not cost him, harness and all, above £32, to White Hall...

117

Detail of William Edney's iron screenwork, 1710, now in southern arch of tower. Photo: Gordon Kelsey.

It was the Admiral's famous Quaker son, William Penn (1644-1718) who, when the government at last settled a debt of £160,000 owed to his father, founded the settlement which he named in his father's honour, Pennsylvania.

If, as far as Redcliffe was concerned, the first Golden Age was the fifteenth century, then the second was the eighteenth century.

In parochial affairs, the legal situation was far different from that prevailing today. The churchwardens of Redcliffe who played so important a part in the history of the building exercised civil as well as ecclesiastical jurisdiction. The Vestry or council of the parish wielded very great powers until as late as 1894, and the present form of Parochial Church Council was not established until 1921. Most of the present-day arrangements and attitudes concerning local government and parochial responsibilities have evolved only in very recent times. The Vestry of a parish such as that of St. Mary Redcliffe had a responsibility for all who lived in the parish and decided on matters of wide concern, such as rates, as well as on purely ecclesiastical matters such as plans to restore the church or commission works of art for its adornment.

By the opening of the eighteenth century the church seems to have been in poor condition. In 1707 the Vestry managed to obtain a 'brief' or royal mandate for a collection to be made throughout all the parishes of England in support of a scheme of restoration and refurbishment: this appeal proved not very successful and in all only about £2,000 was spent. Time has dealt harshly with the efforts of the eighteenth century Vestry. Nowadays their new black and white floor in the choir looks out of place as a setting for the domineering woodwork of the Victorian choir stalls, and similarly the nicely engraved black ledger slabs in the ambulatory around the choir have been re-set in a sea of polychrome Victorian tiles. The several carved monuments erected to the memory of eighteenth century worshippers were banished by the Victorians to the high walls of the tower where few people notice them or can decipher the elegantly phrased inscriptions, so those commemorated tend to be forgotten. Other more substantial furnishings have also suffered the disdain of later generations.

In 1710 William Edney was paid £60 and £50 to make iron gates to close off the chancel and aisles respectively. Parts of this work survive, though now set under the south arch of the tower and on the opposite side of the church in the south nave aisle. Here they can be admired in all their elegance: the gates are, as Sacheverell Sitwell described them, 'one of the splendours of the ignored Baroque art of England'. How effective such transparent work must have been may still be judged, for Robert Bakewell's screen in All Saints, now Derby Cathedral, still survives *in situ*. Later in the century, in 1755, Thomas Paty was paid joinery work so that the font stood in its own specially paved and enclosed space in the north transept. This was the tradition of the Anglican church of the time: to sub-divide a church into parts, for the altar, for baptism, and for the pulpit and congregation.

Other work by Edney in Bristol has also suffered badly, though the gates and sword-rest which he made for St. Nicholas survived the bombing of that church and now adorn a chapel in St. Stephen's. Great gates by Edney can be seen at Elmore Court and at Tewkesbury Abbey, and at Tredegar House, Gwent.

The Vestry Minute Books for October 11th 1726 and March 27th 1727 record the ordering and rebuilding of the organ, with a case to the design of the local architect, John Strahan. The organ was placed against the west wall of the church, and stood in Baroque splendour on a triumphal arch with paired Corinthian columns; the entablature was enriched with garlands and other adornments. The case itself had three great towers for the clusters of larger pipes, rising to a great height to a broken pediment on which angels sat, wings a-flutter. Its loss seems nowadays to be disastrous, and even the Victorians as they decided to remove it in 1867 sensed this. But they thought it 'totally unsuited to the character of the architecture'.

The loss of this organ is also highly regrettable in music terms. It was built by John Byfield, son-in-law of the great Renatus Harris who had died as recently as 1724. In its time the organ had only one rival, that in the newly completed St. Paul's; it was remarkable for its size and complexity, - 26 stops, 1928 pipes - and had 'the first absolutely authentic pedals' in England.

Nowhere in the history of St. Mary Redcliffe are changes in taste so significant as in the sad story of the great altarpiece intended to crown half a century's efforts at embellishing the church. Early in the eighteenth century there was on the high altar a painting by an artist called Holmes: nothing seems to be known of the artist nor much of his painting except that it was obviously considered inadequate to its important situation.

In the Vestry Minutes for May 28th 1755, it is recorded that

It was agreed that the Altar-Piece of the Parish Church of St.

Engraving, City Art Gallery, 1728.

The gallery and magnificent organ.

Mary Redcliff be new painted and that an Application be made to Mr Hogarth to know whether he will undertake to paint the same and to desire him to come from London to survey and make an estimate thereof...

By 1755 William Hogarth was well established as a portrait painter and also as the author of the modern *Moral Subjects and Comic History Paintings*: *Marriage à la Mode* dates from about 1743, the Election series from about 1754. But Hogarth was also intent on raising the professional status of the artist and educating the taste of the English public to accept the Grand Manner in painting. His ideas had been presented in *The Analysis of Beauty*, published by the end of 1753.

That Hogarth accepted the commission indicates its importance to the artist. The only of his other works to bear immediate comparison are the *Pool of Bethesda*, and *The Good Samaritan*, painted in 1736-37 for St. Bartholomew's Hospital, London, and the *St. Paul before Felix*, 1748, intended for the chapel of Lincoln's Inn.

Hogarth painted the three huge canvases in London; the frames however were designed and made in Bristol under the direction of the local architect, Thomas Paty, who also designed the white marble font which still survives in the church. The frames were gilded at the cost of £126 by a local minor painter, John Simmons, whose portrait of one of the Vestrymen, John Watkins, is in the City Art Gallery as well as an Annunciation for All Saints. Hogarth himself received on August 14th 1756 the sum of £525 for his three paintings.

Alas, about one hundred years later, on May 2nd 1853, the Vestry decided to sell the paintings. The tide of taste had turned. It was proposed that the church should be restored, at an estimated cost of £1,500, and the ambulatory behind the high altar was to be restored to use. Hogarth's paintings were disposed of for a nominal sum. In 1859 they were deposited in the Bristol Fine Art Academy, later re-named the Royal West of England Academy. In 1910 another attempt was made to sell the paintings, and when this failed they were rolled up and put in store.

Almost a century after being thrown out of the church, in 1955, the paintings were transferred to the City Art Gallery and put on display. Subsequently they have been cleaned and conserved, and they now provide the most impressive feature in St. Nicholas Church, since 1993 a tourist information centre. They look marvellous in the open space of this well-lit building.

What effect the paintings had when they were still in St. Mary Redcliffe is difficult to recapture. Only the central scene was visible down the length of the church for the two wings of the triptych were set opposite each other on the north and south walls of the chancel. James Johnson's watercolour (City Art Gallery, Braikenridge Collection) gives some indication of the effect. The top of the eastern wall, where the great window had been blocked up, was covered by crimson curtains below which was Hogarth's *Ascension*. This stood on top of a classical reredos which included a small painting of *The Raising of Jarius' Daughter*, the work of Henry Tresham, R.A.

It is evident that Hogarth's Bristol altarpiece must have seemed incongruous to the restorers of the Gothic Revival era. Raised arms, startled looks, billowing draperies, landscape settings in an Italianate rococo manner are hardly Church of England taste. Yet there is much in the altarpiece to admire: individual figures are painted convincingly, the colour range and the areas of light and dark in the landscapes and skies are attractive to the eye. But Hogarth never attained in paintings of this scale the happy intricacies of composition which he achieved in his print *Strolling Actresses in a Barn* (1738), in which he parodies so happily every convention of the Grand Manner which he was doing so much to encourage.

The traditions which Hogarth admired were those of Raphael and Poussin, of the Italian baroque: a great tradition which too few English congregations have been educated to enjoy. The failing of the Gothic Revivalists who threw Hogarth's paintings out was that they could admire no art but the Gothic, and even now there are many who prefer the fake Gothic to the genuine Baroque. Yet today there is nothing at the east end of St. Mary Redcliffe so satisfying artistically or visually as the centre-piece of Hogarth's altarpiece, *The Ascension of Christ*. The subject of the painting, and its scale, was entirely appropriate for so significant a situation in the church, and an elevated style was equally apposite.

Though there is no firm evidence to support the tradition that Handel played on the great new organ of St. Mary Redcliffe, a reproduction of Hogarth's *Ascension* has been used as the sleeve-picture of a recording of *Messiah*. Popular taste is curiously ambivalent, for the conventions of the eighteenth century oratorio are as un-British as anything in Hogarth's paintings. Similarly, as will be seen by any visitor to the church today, the very considerable alterations and additions made by the Vestry in the eighteenth century have almost all been undone, and most people would not regret this. Yet the same people would

Detail of the Ascension, *from the Hogarth triptych, 1756, now in the Tourist Information Centre, St. Nicholas Church.*

doubtless think it philistine to pull down even one minor piece of the surviving eighteenth century domestic architecture of Bristol.

The whole context of the Hogarth paintings and other contemporary work in St. Mary Redcliffe is that of Georgian Bristol. The city seems to have increased in prosperity and splendour at an incredible rate, as can best be studied in Dr. Timothy Mowl's *To Build the Second City* (1991). Other records recently edited indicate something of the character of religious life at St. Mary Redcliffe.

From an analysis of Bishop Secker's *Diocese Book* we learn that the vicar of Redcliffe had an income of more than £250 a year - such figures put all the figures for alterations into perspective. The vicar still held Bedminster and Abbot's Leigh as well as St. Thomas. In 1735-37, the vicar, Mr John Gibb, is described as having 'grown incapable of being heard' but he was assisted by a Mr Lionel Oliver who was paid £40 and by a Mr Williams who was paid £20. In all, Hogarth's altarpiece cost about £800!

Two services were held on Sundays, prayers every afternoon, but Holy Communion only four times a year. In 1784 the parish consisted of nearly 600 families, 150 of them being Dissenters.

Architecturally the prosperity of the parish is indicated by the construction of Redcliffe Parade, begun in about 1768 but not finally completed until 1800. The facades are plain and unpretentious, but in the last few years have been increasingly recognised as a very important feature of the townscape.

The churchyard was given a pretty balustrade which survives along its western edge above the roaring traffic on Redcliffe Hill. Indeed traffic seems first to have begun to affect the area in the eighteenth century: Redcliffe Gate, which had been rebuilt as recently as 1731, was pulled down in 1771 as it was seen to be an inconvenience to commerce.

The self-confidence of the prosperous families of Bristol in the eighteenth century is still visible in the architecture of many parts of the city. Most of the many churches in the city were, like St. Mary Redcliffe, given classical fittings. There are many memorials, some of national significance as works of art. Many of the churches were rebuilt in part or entirely - All Saints, Christchurch, St. Michael's, St. Nicholas, St. Thomas, - and a new one, St. Paul's, built towards the end of the century.

It was into this overwhelmingly classical world that Thomas Chatterton, by far the most fascinating figure in the post-reformation history of St. Mary Redcliffe, was born, on November 20th 1752.

The Chattertons were almost hereditary sextons to St. Mary Redcliffe. His father was master in a school in Pyle Street which had been founded in 1739 after a petition from the Vestry. His mother apparently used scraps of Redcliffe documents as dressmaker's patterns, and it was the records of the church still kept in the Treasury or upper room above the outer north porch which were to prove a major stimulus to the young boy's imagination.

Some writers claim that when only eleven, while still a boy at Colston's, Chatterton published his first poems, among them a satire in *Felix Farley's Journal*, January 1764, against Joe Thomas, one of the churchwardens of Redcliffe who, after the churchyard cross had been destroyed, used the fragments to make bricks. It is clear that eighteenth century 'improvements' being made by the Vestry involved destruction of medieval features: in 1771 the bishop, Philip Yonge, had to protest to prevent the Canynges monument from being thrown out of the church.

Nonetheless, there was already at mid-century some awakening interest in the Middle Ages, particularly in literary terms. In 1764-65 Horace Walpole had written and published *The Castle of Otranto*, a Gothic tale of horrors, a preposterous and nonsensical entertainment (though no less pleasing to pass the time than a present-day mystery thriller or horror film). But the most scandalous affair of all was more academic, and much more controversial - the publication in 1770 of James Macpherson's *Ossian*, supposedly translated from ancient Gaelic originals: this deceit was soon detected and *Ossian* denounced as fraudulent.

It was in 1768, within this context, that Chatterton began to publish writings which, to use perhaps slightly too strong a word, he had forged. Several 'documents' were claimed to bear an authenticity which in the climate of the age provoked great excitement. In effect, Chatterton attempted to recreate an entirely imaginary fifteenth century world which is in many ways still persuasive, though he used a vocabulary and language and verse-forms which now deceive no one as to their authenticity. Central in this imaginative reconstruction was the great medieval church next to which his family lived and within whose walls he found inspiration. Records in the church chests were verbal and literary but the building itself provided the major stimulus.

The central character, after whom the poems became known, was an entirely fictitious character, Thomas Rowley, supposedly a secular priest at St. John's, and secretary to no less a significant figure in the

Above: *Chatterton's route to St. Mary Redcliffe from Pile Street. Watercolour by T.L.S. Rowbotham, 1826.* Braikenridge Collection, City Art Gallery.

Right: *Henrietta Ward's painting of the young Chatterton at home. A popular exhibit at the Royal Academy in 1873 and now in the City Art Gallery.*

history of St. Mary Redcliffe than William Canynges.

The writing of these works seems to have been begun even while Chatterton was at school and continued as he served a dull apprenticeship under John Lambert, a Bristol attorney.

Some critics and publishers, including notably James Dodsley who rejected the 'ancient poems' proffered to him, were immediately suspicious of the authenticity of the Rowley poems. Horace Walpole, so influential a figure of the literary world in London, at first accepted Chatterton but later rejected him. Walpole's close friends, the poets Thomas Gray and William Mason, were both suspicious, for scholarly reasons, of the newly discovered verses.

The time has perhaps come when modern readers can happily accept that there are discernible influences from Shakespeare and Spenser, disguised by borrowings from now out-dated text books, and then read Chatterton's works without being much upset by the anachronisms. It is possible to read *The Bristowe Tragedy*, or *Onn Oure Ladies Chyrche*, and more especially *Aella: A Tragycall Enterlude* with a good deal of pleasure, not unlike that to be gained from a reading of Thomas Gray's *The Bard* or even some of Scott. Perhaps the best thing Chatterton wrote was *An Excelente Balade of Charitie*.

Chatterton moved to London to seek fame but met rejection. Part of his subsequent reputation rests not on his poetry but on the shortness of his life, for he committed suicide in 1770, aged only seventeen. In his poetry he has been sensed as having found a romantic escape from the miseries of modern life. His suicide, as he remembered the critical reception of *Ossian* and despaired of his own success, caught the imagination of Europe. It stimulated novels, a play by Alfred de Vigny, a forgotten opera by Leoncavallo, sentimental mementoes. In England the most touching memorial to the poet is the small painting now in the Tate Gallery by Henry Wallis, *The Death of Chatterton*, first shown at the Royal Academy in 1856. It is one of the masterpieces of Victorian art.

By now it is probably quite impossible to sort out precisely the extent to which Chatterton misled, consciously or unconsciously, three of his fellow Bristolians on matters of history rather than poetry. Certainly Henry Burgum, George Catcott and most particularly William Barrett, one of the first and most important historians of Bristol and also of St. Mary Redcliffe, appear to later generations to have been gullible and credulous. In broad terms, it is easy to recognise that one young lad was allowed too free a rein with original documents which later generations of historians would have cherished.

Some idea of the intense speculation at the time about the authenticity of both *Ossian* and Chatterton can still be sensed in the works of Boswell and Johnson. Not unexpectedly, several references to the *Ossian* controversy are to be found in the two writers' accounts of their *Tour to the Hebrides* in 1773. As regards Chatterton, the revealing episode is that related in *The Life* for Monday, April 29th 1776. Boswell must still have been smiling to himself as he wrote up his memoirs of their literary pilgrimage:

> Honest Catcot seemed to pay no attention whatever to any objections, but insisted, as an end to all controversy, that we should go with him to the tower of St. Mary, Redcliff, and view it with our own eyes the ancient chest in which the manuscripts were found. To this Dr. Johnson good-naturedly agreed; and though troubled with a shortness of breathing, laboured up a long flight of steps, till we came to the place where the wondrous chest stood. 'There, (said Catcot, with a bouncing confident credulity,) there is the very chest itself.' After this ocular demonstration, there was no more to be said.

In the next chapter we shall again encounter the problems caused for historians by Chatterton. Yet above all it is the reputation of the young poet as it affected the next generation of poets which ought to persuade the uninitiated to sample his works.

In the parish registers of St. Mary Redcliffe one famous page includes the record of the marriage on October 4th 1795 of Samuel Taylor Coleridge and Sarah Fricker; Martha Fricker and Josiah Wade were the witnesses, Benjamin Spry the vicar. On the other side of the same page is the record of Robert Southey's marriage on November 14th to Edith Fricker - a sad wedding with bride and groom parting at the church door. Cottle, the publisher, lent Southey money for both the marriage licence and the ring. Five years later Southey and Cottle were to work together to publish an edition of Chatterton's poems for the benefit of Chatterton's needy sister , Mrs Newton and her daughter - a generous gesture inspired by a love for Chatterton and for St. Mary Redcliffe itself.

It was while Coleridge was resident in Bristol that he added a stanza to his *Monody on the Death of Chatterton*:

O Chatterton! that thou werst yet alive!

129

Sure thou wouldst spread the canvas to the gale,
And love, with us, the tinkling team to drive
O'er peaceful freedom's undivided dale;
And we, at sober eve, would round thee throng,
Hanging, enraptured, on thy stately song!
And greet with smiles the young eyed poesy
All deftly masked, as hoar antiquity.

Not only Coleridge admired him but also such diverse poets as Crabbe and Scott and Byron. Keats wrote a sonnet to his memory and dedicated *Endymion* to him. Keats' premature death, like that of his hero, came to personify the poet tragically cut off. And not for nothing did Wordsworth, in one of his most heartfelt and personal poems *Resolution and Independence: The Leech Gatherer*, write

I thought of Chatterton, the marvellous boy,
The sleepless soul that perished in his pride.

Opinions nowadays are frequently unsympathetic to both the poetry and the memory of Chatterton. So sensational a character, so romantic a view of the middle ages are unacceptable to matter-of-fact readers:

If he could not sell his poems, he should have taken a nine-to-five job.
Shelley Rode: *A Private Life of L.S. Lowry* (1979)

FURTHER READING

J.H. Bettey: *Bristol Churches during the Reformation* (Bristol Branch of the Historical Association, 1979)

K.G. Powell: *The Marian Martyrs and the Reformation in Bristol* (Bristol Branch of the Historical Association, 1972)

M.C. Skeeters: *The Clergy of Bristol c. 1530 - c. 1570* (PhD Thesis, University of Texas at Austin, 1984)

For the visit of Queen Elizabeth I, see

J.H. Bettey: 'Two Tudor Visits to Bristol' (*Bristol Record Society XXXVII* (1985)) esp. pp 6-12

For an account of the school in the Lady Chapel,
J. Vane: *Education and Apprenticeship in Sixteenth Century Bristol* (Bristol Branch

of the Historical Association, 1982); pl. IV illustrates the charter initial, March 21st 1590, for Queen Elizabeth Hospital School.

A useful survey of church furniture 'including royal arms' is

B. Little: *Church Treasures in Bristol* (1979)

For Penn's funeral (and much other local material, including the introduction of pin-making to the benefit of otherwise unemployed youngsters) see

J. Latimer: *Annals of Bristol* (3 vols, reprinted 1970)

For William Penn and the Quaker burial ground in Redcliffe,

R. Mortimer: *Early Bristol Quakerism* (Bristol Branch of the Historical Association 1967)

V. Burranelli: *The King and the Quaker: A Study of William Penn* (University of Pennsylvania, 1962)

L. Street: *An Uncommon Sailor: A Portrait of Admiral Sir William Penn* (1986)

For Edney, see

C.F.W. Dening: *The Eighteenth Century Architecture of Bristol* (1923)

S. Sitwell: *British Architects and Craftsmen* (1945)

For the organ and its case,

W. Ison: *The Georgian Buildings of Bristol* (1952, reprinted 1978)

R.T. Morgan: *St. Mary Redcliffe: A Short Account of its Organs* (1912)

P. Williams: *A New History of the Organ* (1980)

Hogarth's altarpiece is mentioned in most monographs on the artist; see also

M.J.H. Liversidge: *William Hogarth's Bristol Altarpiece* (Bristol Branch of the Historical Association, 1980)

For light on church life in eighteenth century Bristol,

E. Ralph (ed.): 'Bishop Secker's Diocese Book' (*Bristol Record Society XXXVII* (1985))

The bibliography on Chatterton is daunting. For a standard biography and literary study - and a masterpiece in its own right, E.H.W. Meyerstein: *A Life of Thomas Chatterton* (1930)

For a concise essay, B. Cottle: *Thomas Chatterton* (Bristol Branch of the Historical Association, 1962)

The legends and reputation of the poet are explored in L. Kelly: *The Marvellous Boy: The Life and Myth of Thomas Chatterton* (1971).

The very many editions of Chatterton's works have all been superseded by D.S.Taylor: *The Complete Works of Thomas Chatterton: A Bicentenary Edition*

(Oxford, 1971), which is complemented by the same authority's *Thomas Chatterton's Art* (Princeton University Press, 1978).

As evidence of the continuing fascination of the topic, see the novel:

Peter Ackroyd: *Chatterton* (1987)

For a recent assessment: S. Brown: 'The Marvellous Boy': Chatterton Manuscripts in the British Library, in M. Jones (ed.): *Why Fakes Matter: Essays on problems of authenticity* (British Museum 1992), chp. 8

7

VICTORIANS AND RESTORATIONS

I have suffered the scaffolding to remain after the building has been completed. In other words I have shown the reader the steps by which I have come to my conclusions ...

W.H. Prescott: *History of the Conquest of Peru* (1847)

It was in 1789 that William Barrett published *The History and Antiquities of the City of Bristol,* a work so important and so fascinating that it was republished in facsimile in 1982 by Alan Sutton. Barrett himself died shortly after the publication of his book; he had been one of the major believers in the works of Chatterton and once their credibility was questioned, so too was Barrett's *History* and its author attacked with great venom. The full title page included the words

> COMPILED FROM original RECORDS and authentic
> MANUSCRIPTS, In Public Offices or private Hands,
> Illustrated with COPPER-PLATE PRINTS.

To question the authenticity of even one of these documents would involve doubting the validity of the whole of this pioneering work.

Chapter XXIV of this compilation, a chapter of some 40 pages, is devoted to the church and parish of St. Mary Redcliffe, with the last nine pages being given over in all seriousness to Chatterton's mock-medieval fabrication

> An ENTYRLUDE, plaied bie the Carmelyte Freers at
> Maiftre Canynges hys greete howfe, before Maiftre
> Canynges and Byfhoppe Carpenterre, on dedicatynge
> the chyrche of Oure Ladie of Redclefte hight.
> THE PARLYAMENTE OF SPRYTES
> Written bie T. Rowleie and J. Iscan

All this romantic versification was annotated profusely by Barrett with a serious attempt at critical scholarship which now strikes us as preposterous.

The vision which Chatterton and Barrett had of the glories of St. Mary Redcliffe is captured for us still in E.V. Rippingille's painting of 1820 which depicts *The Funeral Procession of William Canynges to St. Mary Redcliffe.* But early in the nineteenth century the true situation was less appealing. The watercolour which John Sell Cotman painted in Bristol in about 1800 - it is now in the British Museum - is one of the most famous images of the earlier stages of the industrial revolution. The venerable old Gothic church which rises above the busy quayside is almost obscured by the billowing clouds of dirty smoke which belch from the glass houses all around it.

The west front: proposed design by John Britton and W. Hosking, 1842.

Thomas Girtin's watercolour, in the City Art Gallery, and several other paintings and prints tend to present a prettier interpretation of the scene. The by now familiar and nostalgic oil of 1825 by James Johnson, also in the City Art Gallery, provides us with a view of the church in its suburban setting, almost idyllic in the sunshine of a summer evening. The church is fortunate to have in the vestry a watercolour of 1831 by W.J. Muller showing the building from the north east, still unrestored, lacking pinnacles and with the great east window still blocked up.

Our knowledge of St. Mary Redcliffe since Chatterton's time, though far from complete, becomes quickly more comprehensive. The first monograph on the church appeared in 1813, the work of the celebrated antiquarian and publisher, John Britton. The title of the book indicates its contents:

> AN HISTORICAL AND ARCHITECTURAL ESSAY RELATING TO
> REDCLIFFE CHURCH BRISTOL: ILLUSTRATED WITH PLANS,
> VIEWS AND ARCHITECTURAL DETAILS: INCLUDING AN
> ACCOUNT OF THE MONUMENTS, AND ANECDOTES OF THE
> EMINENT PERSONS INTERRED WITHIN ITS WALLS: Also an Essay
> on THE LIFE AND CHARACTER OF THOMAS CHATTERTON.

John Britton had achieved fame, which he still enjoys, for his celebrated volume of *The Beauties of England and Wales*, twenty volumes in all, published between 1801 and 1814, as well as the more scholarly *Architectural Antiquities of Great Britain* (1807 onwards). Britton's work, culminating in the subsequent series of *Cathedral Antiquities of England*, set a new standard both for historians and architectural students. It was his fate to depict many of the greatest churches of England as they were just before the onslaught of the Victorian restorers, the very people whom he helped stir into action.

From his preliminary remarks it is clear that Britton did not at all underestimate the difficulties which faced him, notably the character of Chatterton's contributions to the myths surrounding the history of the church. Though superseded as a work of scholarship, Britton's *Redcliffe* remains a book which most Bristol antiquarians might wish to own. Though the texts of his books grow yearly more outdated, his illustrations become comparably more valuable.

Still further signs of an ever-awakening interest in the Gothic parts of St. Mary Redcliffe is indicated by the publication in 1823 in Bristol of a work by James Dallaway, using a pseudonym:

St. Mary Redcliffe from the east, by William Muller, 1831.
Reproduced courtesy the Vestry of St. Mary Redcliffe.
Below: *T.L.S. Rowbotham's version from 1826.* City Art Gallery.

St. Mary Redcliffe in its almost idyllic setting recorded by James Johnson in 1825. City Art Gallery.

𝖂illiam 𝖂yrcestre 𝕽edibibus

NOTICES

OF

ANCIENT CHURCH ARCHITECTURE,

IN THE FIFTEENTH CENTURY

PARTICULARLY IN

𝕭𝕽𝕴𝕾𝕿𝕺𝕷.

WITH

HINTS

FOR PRACTICAL RESTORATIONS.

The major theme is that the church ought to be restored, but against what odds and at what price! The octagonal porch, he writes 'has been frequently dilineated with sufficient accuracy. Greatly, indeed, has its fine filligrain carvings been injured by its vicinity to the ceaseless volcanoes, those numerous glass houses; the corrosion of the air, impregnated, as it is, with coal smoke, having decomposed and blackened the surface...'

'To propose,' he continues 'that this portico should be restored to its pristine beauty, would be to indulge a dream , because, although I am confident that ingenious masons might be found, competent to the undertaking, the funds of the Trustees of the church, do not equal the resources of Parliament [who had recently restored Henry VII's chapel at Westminster]. Besides in a few years, the mischief would recur; and it would be as easy a task to remove Vesuvius, and to set it in the sea, as those pyramids, which, not like other volcanoes, have a certain cessation, but continue to throw out volumes of dense smoke, both by day and night.'

Later, to counter this line of argument, it was pointed out that one does not hesitate to tell a grubby boy to go and wash his face even though it is certain soon to get dirty again.

In the pages of 'William Wyrcestre Redivivus' can be sensed a change of taste based on altered attitudes following the exploration of the cities of France once Napoleon had been defeated. Arguments for the completion of the truncated cone of the spire include comparisons with the octagonal lantern of Rouen as well as of Boston, with Harfleur as well as Louth. Particular mention is made of S. Maclou at Rouen - but such influences did not find fulfilment in Bristol for nearly a century until the University tower was built.

> Would a lover of architectural antiquities, and one who admires the Italian Schools of Painting, be deemed worthy of forgiveness, if he breathed a wish, in silence, that the sum of £761 and one penny, had been applied in preference, to a pious renovation of the former splendour of St. Mary Redcliffe, instead of having been paid to Hogarth for his three Altar pictures?...
>
> When the sublime efforts of the painters of Italy were applied to the decoration of churches, it was of those which were the works of their contemporary architects, and not of the Gothic age; in which the scriptural subjects were universally stained in glass, or painted in fresco. It has therefore excited in my mind, whether modern pictures can be placed in Gothic churches, with that strictness of local appropriation, which must ever be demanded by good taste.

By 1823, it seems, the tide of taste had changed - and as far as this one church is concerned, still runs strongly in the same direction.

The next publication, dating from 1834, is more substantial, a book of just over 200 pages, some of which has already been quoted, and still so important that it cannot be neglected by anyone interested either in medieval Bristol or more specifically in St. Mary Redcliffe. This is James Dallaway's

Antiquities of Bristow

IN THE

Middle Centuries;

INCLUDING

THE TOPOGRAPHY

BY

William Wyrcestre

AND

THE LIFE OF

William Canynges.

The books by Barrett, Britton and James Dallaway together with the earlier visionary work by Chatterton created a climate which affected the costly and long-drawn-out campaigns of restoration and refurbishment undertaken by the Victorians. This is a huge topic and in a restricted space it is possible only to sample the wealth of evidence.

In 1842 the Vestry of St. Mary Redcliffe published a thirty page appeal for subscriptions under the title:

RESTORATION OF THE CHURCH OF SAINT MARY REDCLIFFE
BRISTOL: AN APPEAL BY THE VICAR, CHURCHWARDENS, AND
VESTRY; WITH AN ABSTRACT OF REPORTS BY MESSRS.
BRITTON AND HOSKING; AND ENGRAVED PLAN AND VIEWS OF
THE CHURCH.

John Britton we have already met; William Hosking (1800-1861) was an engineer who at this time was Professor of the Arts of Construction and Professor of the Principles and Practice of Architecture at King's College, London.

This Appeal book reads much as does any similar work, with all the familiar words and phrases which lead up to the crucial words on costing 'with a due estimate for contingencies, in works so extensive, and of such comparatively novel character, cannot, in the judgement of the Parish Authorities, be safely calculated at a sum much less than £40,000.'

This sum was to include the reconstruction of the spire, and the re-ordering of the church interior which is discussed in the following terms:

A learned and travelled clergyman who has devoted some years to the study of the church architecture of the middle ages ... laments the effects of Hogarth's pictures with their vulgar draperies, and the filling in of the east window and of the altar-screen beneath; and reprobates the barbarous and lofty pews which cut up and destroy much of the architectural beauty of the Church.

Fortunately for the cause of architecture and good taste, we are living in times when the enlightened higher orders of the clergy appreciate the beauties of the ancient churches in which they officiate; and when not only Deans and Archdeacons but many Churchwardens, consider it to be a pleasure as well as a

The spire completed, 1872. Reece Winstone Collection.

duty to render willing aid in upholding and preserving, while they really adorn, the sacred edifices committed to their care. Hence the contrast between this and a former age is striking, and, at the same time, truly gratifying to all admirers of ancient architecture.

It was planned also to 'set a laudable example' and move all the memorials from the pillars and from the sides of windows and 'arrange with some attention to simplicity and symmetry'. The effects which were to be achieved were indicated by the exquisite engraved views of both exterior and interior views of the church in its hoped-for pristine condition, spire rising into a clear and sunny sky, the interior empty of all pews and monuments and free of the despised paintings by Hogarth.

Nowadays searchers for eighteenth century monuments will find a group of them gathered together under the tower, all inscriptions and urns, cherubic faces and skulls. What a contrast there is, and indicative of the earlier phases of Gothic Revival in Redcliffe on the eve of the Victorian restoration of the church, in the two Gothic cenotaphs of the eastern wall of the north transept.

One, consisting of a single gabled and pinnacled tabernacle, was erected to the memory of George Wyld and his wife who died in 1834 and 1820 respectively; the other is grander, in tripartite form and with pedestals for statuary. This is to the memory of Nathaniel Bridge, lecturer of the parish, and was erected in 1835.

The men who built the spire, photographed in 1872.
Reece Winstone Collection.

Sadly visitors to Redcliffe can no longer enjoy the most significant essay in this early style of Gothic Revival, the 'kind of Eleanor Cross' erected in 1840 to the memory of Thomas Chatterton to a design by S.C. Fripp. This memorial had a chequered history, for a while being banished from the churchyard by one vicar since the poet had committed suicide. This monument was, alas, demolished as recently as 1967. As a work of art it was perhaps more curious and amusing than beautiful, but it did nonetheless represent a serious, and locally significant, effort of a generation which hardly understood the true principles of Gothic architecture. Perhaps the weakest element of the whole design was the figure itself, too small a doll, dressed as a Colston School boy, holding a scroll of his tragedy, *Aella*.

Of the quite extensive works of these decades, even more completely forgotten is the extension and remodelling, in a sort of Gothic, of the organ gallery with niches and gabling and crockets much like the surviving cenotaphs and lamented Chatterton monument. This work, carried out in 1840, lasted only until 1866-67 when the organ was split into two parts and placed at either side of the choir. It was further re-arranged in 1910 and again, after a fire caused by intruders, in 1947.

The temptation to relate the history of St. Mary Redcliffe within the context of the complex history of the Gothic Revival, and of the Oxford Movement, must be resisted; but we ought at least to recall the date of one of the major polemic publications of the movement, 1841 - the year of A.W. Pugin's

CONTRASTS: OR, A PARALLEL BETWEEN THE WHOLE EDIFICES OF
THE MIDDLE AGES, AND CORRESPONDING BUILDINGS OF THE
PRESENT DAY; SHEWING THE PRESENT DECAY OF TASTE...

The text of the book is as vehement as the title, and so are the paired illustrations. The most famous and most frequently reproduced pair, the view of a 'Catholic Town in 1440' and 'THE SAME TOWN IN 1840' might almost be views of Bristol as seen from Redcliffe or Temple Meads, a view of warehouses, bottle-furnaces and smoking chimneys. The first pair of illustrations is of the classical reredos and baroque altarpiece then in Hereford Cathedral contrasted with the Neville Screen in Durham Cathedral - so absurd a contrast and so persuasive, between a piece of artisan baroque and one of the masterpieces of Gothic England. On the next page, equalling the previous comparison in its persuasiveness are shown a Georgian street scene with John

Detail from Rowbotham's panoramic view of Bristol
from Pile Hill, c. 1829. City Art Gallery.
Below *John Sell Cotman watercolour, c.1800.* The British Museum.

Victorian Bristol from the tower of St. Mary Redcliffe.

Nash's church of All Souls, Langham Place and, in unfair competition, great processions and catholic ceremonial taking place outside the north porch, the broad west front and soaring spire of St. Mary Redcliffe.

In fact the clear view of the church from the north, a view with which we are all now so familiar, was one of the earliest ' improvements', carried out soon after 1842, as recorded in a statement by John Britton:

> ...This edifice has been completely insulated in its north elevation, raised on a terrace, is fully exposed to the inspection of every passing traveller - and presents a facade of unparalleled richness, intricacy and natural beauty, thertofore, even in the days of its pristine splendour we may believe that this was scarcely if at all seen; but now, by the good sense of the Corporation in taking away old and ruinous houses and making a broad street and spacious area, every part of this unique architectural design, both in elevation and at different angular points, are commended and seen by the admirer of ecclesiastical buildings. A still greater improvement is now in progress, by removing an old wall and taking away ground and rubbish to the depth of 4 or 5 feet at the immediate base of the Church, and sloping then to the level street below...

No better record of church life in Bristol could be hoped for than is found in a series of articles reprinted in book form as *The Church Goer being a series of Sunday Visits to the Various Churches of Bristol*, published in 1845. The book reveals much, some distressing, some amusing as at Redcliffe:

> I don't know whether or not parish clerks may be out of my province; if it were not taking a liberty, however, I would meekly beg that the rev. the vicar might ... devote a spare hour to teaching his clerk to deport himself with more reverend humility in his business: he lolled upon his left hand in an air of the utmost complacency, and casting a sidelong glance towards the ceiling said 'We beseech thee to hear us, good Lord,' as if it did not greatly concern him whether his prayers were complied with or not.

Such records, and they become increasingly comprehensive, indicate the slow and spasmodic progress of the Victorian restoration of the church: it was not effected speedily, nor without interruptions, nor without considerable financial difficulties. Work continued in all through more than thirty years, between 1846 and 1877, under the control of the highly respected editor of the influential periodical, *The Builder*, George Godwin. Until his resignation due to increasing age in 1848, he was aided by John Britton.

A number of reports and other publications supplement the evidence still visible in the church marking the progress of the work. Godwin's own attitude is summarised in a booklet published by Jefferies in 1846: in a speech the architect emphasised the seriousness of his responsibilities in words which are still valid. '...St. Mary Redcliffe,' he emphasised, 'belonged not simply to Bristol but to Europe...'

By now the earliest of the many Victorian memorial windows were being put in. Mr Wailes did an east window 'universally admired'; and in December 1854 a Ladies' Window in the south transept at the cost of £200. Mr Bell, the Bristol glazier, reassembled pieces of ancient glass for a transept window at the cost of £25. But it is recorded that in 1855, a period of low ebb in finances, other windows had to be left with only canvas. The pamphlet *Sixteen Years Doings in the Restoration of St. Mary Redcliffe Church* published in 1858 is very revealing. Plans were being made to move the organ and then restore the large west window of the nave. But the work already done was by now provoking criticism; the new work shone so crisp next the crumbling unrestored parts. A critic recognised the danger and possibilities - 'it is possible to replace the ancient structure which is now crumbling on Redcliffe Hill with a perfect FACSIMILE of its original proportions...'

In 1922 Sir Harold Brakspear published his own study of the church which opens with words which still remain appropriate:

> Words cannot express the feeling of indignation at the ruthless desecration that has been perpetrated in the cause of so-called restoration, even fifty years after the mischief has been done.

For the architectural historian one of the distressing features of the Victorian restoration is the thoroughness with which the masons worked and their almost complete failure to record what they discovered, what they replaced and what they invented. Some features are discussed sensibly in the many, rather repetitive articles and books by George Pryce on the architectural history of the whole city.

The names of many of the patrons of the restoration work are recorded, and today most obviously in the dedicatory panels of the succession of stained glass windows. Several of the families still flourish in Bristol though most of the firms which they led no longer survive. But by far the most significant patron was Thomas Proctor, Chairman of the Appeal, who under the pseudonym 'Nil Desperandum' provided the money for the repair of the north porch and is still remembered for having 'greatly encouraged the work'.

The mason in charge of the work on the north porch and for much other carving was a Mr William Rice who had earlier worked on Hereford Cathedral. Initially he was paid £2.15s. a week, but by 1854-55, when he supervised a team of fourteen or fifteen, he earned £184 a year. One of the most appealing images of the period is the photograph which shows a group of the restorers stiffly posed outside the church. A personal touch was afforded by the discovery during the restoration work of the 1930s of a note tucked into the carving of a roof boss, recording the names of masons working on July 2nd 1875. Their wages were 8 1/2d. an hour when beef cost 1/- a pound and a four pound loaf 5d.

Among the church treasures, along with plate and documents, are the ceremonial trowel and mallet used to celebrate the completion of the spire in 1872. Rising to 292 feet, the spire is now more important even than when it was first rebuilt, and overtops even most of the new office-block towers. There are interesting photographs of the work in progress in Reece Winstone's book *Bristol as it was, 1874-1866*. Almost as ˙ important as the spire in altering the whole effect of the exterior was the reconstruction of the many pinnacles which mark each bay of both aisle and clerestory. They are very telling in the way they reinforce the verticals of the building, as can be seen by looking for comparison at any of the many illustrations made before about 1850. Yet, as in June 1984 when one of the pinnacles began to sway dangerously in a strong wind and threatened to fall through the north nave aisle, it is easy to understand how one might say 'Let's take them all off before they cause a lot of damage'.

If one tries, a century after the Victorians, to identify what it is about St. Mary Redcliffe that gives it such a reputation, one is forced, perhaps a little unwillingly, to admit that this reputation was greatly stimulated by the impact of Chatterton's writings on subsequent generations. But the reputation is based on something wider than this. Most English writers, critics, travellers, worshippers and pilgrims have rejected the ideals of the classical and baroque. English popular taste is for the picturesque, and even among the greatest of English Gothic buildings few are more picturesque than St. Mary Redcliffe. Where the Palladian country house is ordered and the Georgian terrace in its square all symmetrical, St. Mary Redcliffe is all asymmetrical, angular and animated. All the popular souvenir views of the church emphasise its most picturesque features, the flying buttresses and niches, the gables and pinnacles, and rising above them all the spire.

All these elements which are now taken for granted were in fact all remade and paid for by the Victorians. The difficulties which they had to overcome were many; raising money was a continuing headache, and knowing how to proceed sensibly was always far from easy. As the reports in the local press indicate, the thirty or more years of restoration were years of worry and intermittent controversy.

One of the most significant, and still most famous, achievements of the Victorians was the installation of the noble full ring of twelve bells; the bells were recast in 1903 and rehung in 1933. But the history of Redcliffe bells is much longer. A bell foundry existed in the parish as early as 1296. In 1451 a certain Hew the Bellman is recorded in Redcliffe when he was paid iij li. i ii s. by the parish of Yatton, Somerset: Hew's foundry clearly had a good reputation. When William Worcestre recorded what he found at St. Mary Redcliffe he included the weights of six bells. Bells were rung, it is recorded in the Mayor's Audits, at the time of the mayor's visits in 1532 and 1533. In 1636 there were only four bells but these had been increased to eight by 1689. Bristol has long been notable for its many rings of bells, as acknowledged by the names of Bristol Surprise Major and Clifton Surprise Royal; the Bristol United Guild was also far-famed for the generosity of its dinners. They are celebrated in the poetry of John Betjeman, and there is indeed poetry in the ancient inscriptions on the Redcliffe bells:

(3) PROSPERITY TO OUR BENEFACTORS

(5) YOU MEE TRY RING: ILE SWEETLY SING: AR: 1698

[AR are the initials of Abraham Rudhall.]

(11) DRAWE NEARE TO GOD

(12) COME WHEN I CALLE TO SERVE GOD ALL

1622: T.S: IE. T.P.C.W.

while on the bell-cage is recorded

151

T.ROOME . OF . THIS . CITTIE . CARPENTER . ANNO . DOMINIE .
1636 . JAMES . WARTHING . JOHN . READ . CHURCH WARDENS .

It is in the interior of the church that the Victorian contributions are most obviously Victorian. The new fittings include a complete spread of brightly patterned tiles the design of which is as characteristic of their age as is the prodigious central heating system incorporating gratings with Gothic detailing and bundles of pipework proudly signed and dated V. SKINNER 1874.

All the new woodwork, including a full set of choir stalls, a pulpit with carvings of the apostles (like the medieval one at Trull), robust pews with doors for a large congregation and a draught-proof porch to enclose the south door, was designed by Godwin and carved by a Mr William Bennett of Portishead. The arrangement of all this stolid, darkly stained woodwork owes little to medieval precedent and is now thought by many to be something of a hindrance to modern fashions in liturgy. As some of the Victorian writers realised, St. Mary Redcliffe has never been an ideal shape for modern services which seem to demand the open centralised form as used for All Saints or the Roman Catholic Cathedral in Pembroke Road rather than a long, eastward looking interior.

The saddest feature of the interior is the way in which the bulk of the pipe-work of the organ still makes for bottlenecks in the choir aisles, darkening the western bays of the choir and blocking the diagonal views across the eastern arm of the church.

Many details of the final stages of the restoration are documented by stray references but however hard one tries to put together such ephemeral notes, nothing in the end seems to challenge the accounts written by the archaeologist and vicar of St. Mary Redcliffe, Canon J.P. Norris who published in volume 3 (1878) of the but-newly founded Bristol and Gloucester Archaeological Society's *Transactions* his 'Notes on St. Mary Redcliffe', and a book in 1882.

Finally in our consideration of the Victorian work on and in the church we come to the stained glass. It is impossible to ignore it. The best of the first phase, 1854, is at the east end of the south choir aisle; that at the opposite end of the church, at the end of the south nave aisle, is very lively when the sun reaches it later in the afternoon.

Most of the windows - by Bell of Bristol, or Clayton and Bell - conform to consistent programmes and overall designs: none is downright bad,

The high altar, with Victorian reredos. Photo: Veale.

none of great note. The intrusive windows are the Pre-Raphaelite ones recently moved down from the clerestory to fill a gap in the eastern aisle of the south transept, and the pale Comper window (1910) in the great south window next to it.

Opinions of previous writers are often contradictory. Edith Williams, in her 1931 *Guide*, was not critical but Basil Cottle in his of 1957 was witty in his disapproval. The present writer feels that the side clerestory windows of the choir do little except reduce the light-levels of that part of the church while the nave looks better with clear glazing at clerestory level; to remove windows at eye-level would provide distracting views of parts of Bristol that have little to commend them.

The Victorian restorers had to contend with the neglect of the fabric over three centuries and the increasing damage caused by industrial pollution. It was the continuing effects of pollution and the use of unsuitable materials by the Victorians which necessitated the major reparations to the fabric carried out under the direction of Sir George Oatley during the years 1927-33. The exterior was restored under the patronage of Sir Gilbert Wills, first Lord Dulverton, the interior (which had become very blackened) by the newly re-constituted Canynges Society. This restoration was fully celebrated in a special series of services and by the publication of an invaluable little book, Cecil Powell's *St. Mary Redcliffe Church: An Account of the Great Service of Thanksgiving for the Restoration on November 3rd, 1933 and Other Matters.*

It was in the 1930s that Miss Edith Williams began publishing the results of her researches while Archivist to the church; her work included the invaluable guidebook mentioned earlier and culminated in her major book on the Chantries published in 1950.

So much good work was done on the church in the period just before the war that it is saddening to recall that in 1937 one of the most significant buildings in the area, Canynges's House, was pulled down. Its loss is irremediable. Work of the same period culminated in the dedication of the new undercroft and steps before the north porch on May 5th 1940.

Pollution and decay necessitated a further major series of campaigns of restoration costing £150,000, in the years 1960-65. By the 1990s the church which twenty five years earlier had looked so clean had become grimy again, and thoughts were turning towards the next restoration.

FURTHER READING

Benjamin Hickey's *City Plan* (1743) shows glass-houses to the east as well as to the west of the church; for a history of the glass industry in Bristol, and for the little-known Prewitt Street glass-house (now part of the Bristol Hilton hotel) see C. Witt, C. Weedon and A.P. Schwind: *Bristol Glass* (1984).

For John Britton and the wider context, see N. Pevsner: *Some Architectural Writers of the Nineteenth Century* (1972); Britton's statement, quoted above, is in manuscript in the Central Reference Library on College Green.

For George Godwin, 1815-1888 see *Dictionary of National Biography.* G. Godwin: 'The North Porch of Redcliffe Church': *The Builder* VII (January 1st 1849) has a fine plate. Among his other works is the polygonal Gothic fountain now on the green near the Mansion House in Clifton, for which and the whole context see Clare Crick's invaluable *Victorian Buildings in Bristol* (1975).

H.T. Ellacombe: *The Church Bells of Gloucestershire* (1881) lists the bells of Bristol including St. Mary Redcliffe.

For Hew the Bellman, of Redcliffe (and much more of interest) see *Yatton Churchwardens' Accounts*: Somerset Record Soc. IV (1890).

APPENDIX: The Church Cat

Most great churches have something special. Many visitors to St. Mary Redcliffe search eagerly for the memorial slab inscribed THE CHURCH CAT 1912-1927. This can be found in the churchyard near the south transept.

But why is it so famous? Perhaps for historical reasons; for example Arthur Bryant: *The Years of Endurance, 1793-1802*, found space in a history of England to describe a riot in London when a lady had her cat buried in hallowed ground; two hours after its interment the corpse was flung through her window.

The Redcliffe memorial is not unique; indeed, at Fairford, Glos. a church cat is commemorated by a sculpted monument: see *Country Life* 90 (1941), p. 337. There is a cat cemetery outside the south east cloister door at Salisbury Cathedral.

But connoisseurs of the by-ways of ecclesiological ephemera will be enchanted to know that there are bibliographical references to pursue:

Stephen Richards (grandson of Eli Richards, Verger 1905-1925): *St Mary Redcliffe: The Church Cat (1912-1927)*, (2pp., price 8p, my copy annotated August, 1988).

For a photograph of the cat, Tom, and the verger, see G.M. Spriggs: 'Cats at Home in Church', *Country Life*, December 28th 1976. N. Orme: *Exeter Cathedral as it was, 1050-1550* (1986) records payments for cats in the cathedral, and a cat hole in a door in the north transept.

CONCLUSION

The Church of England has traditionally sought to maintain a balance between the old and the new.

Preface to *The Alternative Service Book* (1980)

The air raids of 1939-1945 afflicted the parish very seriously: the length of tram-line embedded in the churchyard after being blown sky-high serves as a reminder of how close the church came to destruction. St. John Bedminster, to which St. Mary Redcliffe had been historically linked, was completely destroyed. It had been rebuilt in 1855 but its fifteenth century font had survived and in 1983 it was placed in the tower of St. Mary Redcliffe for safe-keeping - a significant gesture of the continuity of traditions within the Church.

Other episodes in the artistic history of the church are more puzzling. When Hogarth's altar paintings had been thrown out, a brand new reredos in the Gothic style was placed behind the High Altar: its form is recorded in photographs. But as early as 1871 this was considered to be unsatisfactory, and it was replaced by a much grander affair designed by Godwin and carved in Caen stone by Rice. In the centre was the *Crucifixion*, flanked by the *Way to Calvary* and the *Angel at the Tomb*; these scenes were set beneath pinnacled gables which led the eye upwards and provided a visual link between the High Altar and the great east window above it. Alas, this reredos was in its turn thrown out in 1975, opening up a vista which distracts attention from the High Altar. At this time, it was suggested in the local press that the chance ought to be taken to return the Hogarth paintings to the church for which they were created...

Since 1965 the eye has been further distracted by the bold colours of the new glass by H.J. Stammers which fills the Lady Chapel with light of a quality quite unlike that of any other part of the building. Indeed it is quite a culture shock to enter this refurbished room. Having become acclimatised to Victorian dark stained woodwork, Victorian polychrome tiles, Victorian windows, one treads on pale wall-to-wall carpet and sits on chaste modern chairs. The same sort of restrained 'good taste' is apparent in the refurnishing of the chapel created by American Friends of St. Mary Redcliffe in 1962-65 in the space under the tower. The design of the altar frontal is depressingly weak, especially beneath the medieval glass of the west window.

Saddest of all is the way in which over the last half century or so almost all of the ancient setting of the proud church has been systematically destroyed.

The date of the wide access thoroughfare cut to provide a link between Bristol Bridge and Temple Meads Station is proclaimed by its name, Victoria Street. Beyond Temple Meads are the roads to Wells and the south west, and to Bath and London. The huge disaster as far as the immediate surroundings of the church is concerned was the creation of the Inner Ring Road, Redcliffe Way, planned in the 1930s, and bringing heavy traffic along the north side of the church. The new bridge across the Avon towards Queen Square, which until its partial closure in the 1990s was also ravished by heavy traffic, bears on it the date of its opening, 1942.

Redcliffe parish suffered heavily in the war, but the character of the immediate environment of the church was further damaged by the widening of Redcliffe Hill, involving the destruction of several interesting buildings, including William Watt's shot tower.

> St. Mary Redcliffe is now a traffic island; you have to be nippy to reach it without injury... The grave yard has very few tombstones; either everyone opted for willow-trees or else the dead have been tidied... From the north steps I could see Chatterton's house sticking up like a tooth in the gum of the motorway. It's a wonder the traffic hasn't shaken it loose.
>
> Beryl Bainbridge: *English Journey* (1984)

The parish churches of England are amongst our national treasures the most loved, the most studied and yet most at risk. Though the industries of Redcliffe are now less noisome than in the eighteenth and nineteenth centuries, the traffic which roars all round the church deafens the bells and the organ, threatening more damage than the reformers, causing more pollution that the glass-houses. Traffic threatens the efforts of many generations of men and women of Redcliffe who over the centuries have sought to preserve it as an inspiration for future generations.

In the last few years huge changes have been begun in the redevelopment of the commercial and domestic environment of the church. There are new offices and new blocks of flats both eastwards towards Temple Meads and westwards along the quayside. At last the whole area between the church and Bristol Bridge, a part of Bristol which has been a disgrace and a mess for about a century, has been recognised as having potential.

The features which combine to give St. Mary Redcliffe a reputation of superlatives are varied. One of the major interests of the building is its long and fascinating history. It is one of the most significant monuments of piety in one of the most historic of English cities, for centuries a centre of artistic patronage, devotion and worship.

From whichever angle one approaches it, the exterior of the church is very impressive. If present hopes are fulfilled and a square is created to the north of the church, it will be more of a pleasure to admire the north side of the building. The Decorated outer north porch and contrasting Early English inner porch provide an amazingly lively experience which does not dim however often one enters the church:

> Since I am coming to that Holy room
> Where, with thy Quire of Saints for evermore,
> I shall be made thy Music; as I come
> I tune the instrument here at the door...

On the other side of the church, the tranquillity of the south wall, with the sun shining across the green churchyard, reminds one of the original parochial setting.

The Victorian rebuilding of the spire must be accounted a great success; its height pulls together the length of the nave and choir and Lady Chapel with the spreading transepts into a single composition. The weathercock, and the bells more noisily, attract attention from afar, above the roofs of offices, even above the roar of the traffic.

It is amazing how well integrated is the architecture of the interior even though it is the work of so long a succession of patrons and masons working spasmodically in a long sequence of campaigns over so many centuries. That the interior is darkened and a good deal cluttered by Victoriana is one of the more problematic aspects confronting the present generation.

The church has a marvellous rhythm in the way its tall succession of open arcades support the vertical panelling and clerestory windows above which soar the vaults in all their intricate variety. St. Mary Redcliffe is not a church to be taken in at a glance; in opening up a vista past the High Altar the whole aesthetic of the building has been disturbed. The church is as complex in its spaces as it is in its history: to judge it as if it were a cinema or theatre is to misjudge it entirely. The least felicitous view inside the church, sad to admit, is that from the nave, where most of the congregation sit, towards the high altar; there is no focus for the eye, only a tangle of jarring lines and clashing colours. The finest views are diagonally across the church, from the nave aisles to the opposite transept or, depending on the light, from near the alabaster effigy of Canynges back towards the north door. One of the major characteristics of Gothic is variety, and in these terms St.

Mary Redcliffe is a masterpiece.

In recent years the high vaults have been redecorated, and the church has celebrated the four hundredth anniversary of the return to the church by Queen Elizabeth I of lands confiscated at the dissolution of the chantries. Local children have taken part in a new venture, exploring in excited workshop-groups for a whole day many aspects of the history and traditions and life of this great church.

The study of the history of St. Mary Redcliffe suggests that its future is likely to prove challenging. Though there may yet be still more delays, there is the prospect that in the mid-1990s major improvements will be made to the roadway, with the primary aim of distancing the traffic from the north side of the church.

Whatever the future holds, the building will ever be busy with visitors - not just from Henleaze on the other side of Bristol but also from France, Germany, Italy, Switzerland, from the United States and from the other side of the world, Australia. St. Mary Redcliffe has a place in the history of Bristol, and a reputation which circles the globe.

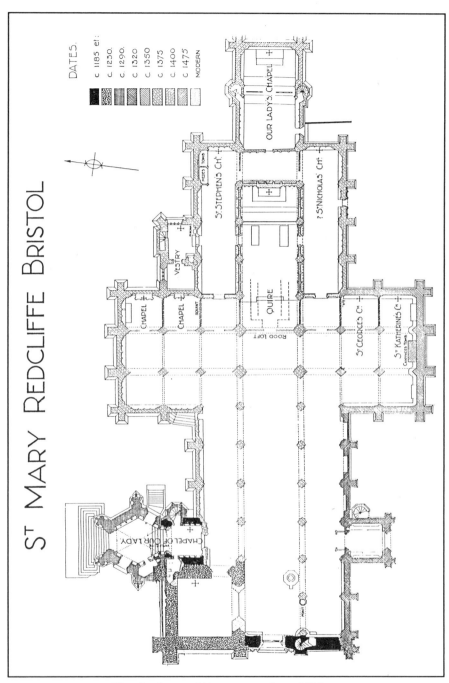

St Mary Redcliffe Bristol

DATES.

c. 1185 et:
c. 1250.
c. 1290.
c. 1320.
c. 1350
c. 1375
c. 1400
c. 1475
MODERN

OUR LADY'S CHAPEL

St STEPHEN'S Ch.

? St NICHOLAS' Ch.

VESTRY

CHAPEL

CHAPEL

QUIRE

ROOD LOFT

St GEORGE'S Ch.

St KATHERINE'S Ch.

CHAPEL OF OUR LADY

The Oatley and Lawrence plan, 1922.

CHRONOLOGICAL GLOSSARY

The following terms are among the most frequently used to describe English medieval architecture.

ROMANESQUE is a round-arched style, used by the Romans and adopted by the Anglo-Saxons; since it was dominant for about a century after the Norman Conquest it is often called ANGLO-NORMAN. It was subject to many regional variations particularly in the west country in the period c. 1150-75, when several features including the POINTED ARCH and RIB VAULTING (i.e. vaults strengthened with diagonal ribs) indicate a TRANSITIONAL phase when architecture seems to be evolving towards the GOTHIC. The most significant innovations - especially the use of FLYING BUTTRESSES to allow solid wall to be replaced by windows - were made in France (e.g. St. Denis , 1142, and Chartres).

In England local characteristics, as at Wells and Salisbury, suggested the term EARLY ENGLISH (c. 1175-1250). The cutting of capitals with non-naturalistic foliage is characteristic, and known as STIFF LEAF; when the leaves are deeply under-cut and in lively form they are known as WIND-BLOWN. Shafts are often of a local 'marble', such as PURBECK, or in Wells and Bristol, the local blue lias. The bases to shafts are often concentric and cut into deep WATER-HOLDING forms. Windows are single with pointed tops, LANCETS; when two are arranged together with a smaller, usually circular one above, this is known as PLATE TRACERY. After c. 1250 TRACERY of cut stone is used to create windows of many lights; vertical elements are called MULLIONS, the horizontals are TRANSOMS.

In the last quarter of the thirteenth century tracery becomes less GEOMETRICAL and more and more CURVILINEAR or FLOWING. DECORATED is the term used for the style dominant after c. 1290. A regular feature is a double-curved form known as an OGEE; when it occurs in three-dimensional form it is known as a NODDING OGEE. Vaults often have more than four ribs: extra ribs are called TIERCERONS; minor, non-structural ribs are often added between the tiercerons, LIERNES which often form STAR or STELLAR vaults. At the junction of the ribs the key-stones or BOSSES are often richly carved. Naturalistic foliage is characteristic of Decorated. Ribs in vaults, and arches, are often enriched with subsidiary projecting points, like thorns on a rose, known as CUSPS.

Such extravagances were restrained in the PERPENDICULAR (c. 1340 onwards) when the emphasis was on repetitive, four-square panelling, with vertical lines which often pass across the curves of arches. Horizontal features are often given crenellations or MACHICOLATIONS. In the Perpendicular the carving of capitals on piers and RESPONDS (the half-pier built with the wall) is less florid than in the Decorated, and bases are frequently polygonal.

SELECT BIBLIOGRAPHY

A very large collection of books, guidebooks, articles and other more ephemeral items about the church is accessible at the Central Reference Library on College Green. The major pictorial archive, including especially items from the Braikenridge Collection, is at the City Art Gallery; selections from this collection are displayed from time to time.

The major collection of original documents is in the archives of St. Mary Redcliffe: see I. Gray and E. Ralph: *Guide to the Parish Records of the City of Bristol and County of Gloucester* (Bristol and Gloucester Archaeological Society, 1963), pp 22-23.

The following list of books, pamphlets and articles includes only those of major importance and is arranged in chronological order: they include much omitted from the present book.

William Barrett: *The History and Antiquities of the City of Bristol* (1789, reprinted 1982), esp. chap. XIV

John Britton: *An Historical and Architectural Essay relating to Redcliffe Church, Bristol* (1813)

James Dallaway: *Antiquities of Bristow in the Middle Centuries; including the Topography of William Worcestre and the Life of William Canynges* (1834)

George Pryce: *Notes on the Ecclesiastical and Monumental Architecture and Sculpture of the Middle Ages in Bristol* (1850)

J.F. Nichols and J. Taylor: *Bristol Past and Present*, vol II (1881), pp 195-219

J.P. Norris: *Some Account of the Church of St. Mary Redcliffe* (1882)

Harold Brakspear: 'St. Mary Redcliffe, Bristol'; *Transactions of the Bristol and Gloucester Archaeological Society XLIV* (1922), pp 2 71-292, with the standard plan.

E.W. Meyerstein: *A Life of Chatterton* (1930)

Edith Williams: *St. Mary Redcliffe, Bristol* (1931)

Cecil Powell and others: *St. Mary Redcliffe Church* (1933)

Edith Williams: *The Chantries of William Canynges in St. Mary Redcliffe* (1950)

Nikolaus Pevsner: *North Somerset and Bristol* (The Buildings of England, 1958)

R.F. Cartwright: *The Pictorial History of St. Mary Redcliffe* (Pitkin Pride of Britain, 1963)

A. Gomme, M. Jenner and B. Little: *Bristol: An Architectural History* (1979)

J. Bony: *The English Decorated Style* (1979)

J. Sherborne: *William Canynges 1402-1474* (Bristol Branch of the Historical Association, 1985)

FURTHER LISTENING

A recital by Garth Benson: The Organ in St. Mary Redcliffe V P S 1045 Stereo

Change ringing from St. Mary Redcliffe SAYDISC 243 Stereo

These may be obtained from the church bookstall, as well as the current all-colour guidebook, a short guide, a children's guide, and a variety of slides, post cards and other souvenirs.

THE CANYNGES SOCIETY

This society, the Friends of St. Mary Redcliffe, membership of which is open to all, was founded in 1848, disbanded in 1873 and refounded in 1927. It aims to provide funds for the preservation, improvement and refurbishment of the church.

INDEX

Page numbers in bold relate to illustrations

SUBSCRIBERS

Bryan and Ann Anderson
Simon M. Andrew
Kenneth C. Aplin
David Campbell Ayers
Michael Baber
Derek Bond
Bristol Grammar School
Bristol Museums & Art Gallery
Michael Leonard Brooks
T.H.B. Burrough
Dr. Geoffrey W. Burton
Christine Bush
The Right Rev'd R.F.
  Cartwright
The Venerable K.J. Clark
Ronald Cleak
Norman and Donald Cornish,
  grandsons of the late Rev'd
  Charles Edward Cornish
Derek and Kate Day
Ald. Claude Draper
Glyn and Joy Duggan
John Bennett Dunn
R.R. Emanuel
David and Moira Felce
Mrs. Elizabeth Fletcher
Peter John Floyd
Mrs. Sheila M.M. Forster
Dr. & Mrs. Dennis H. Fox
Miss J.M. Fraser
The Very Reverend David
  Frayne

Miss Cecile Gillard
Francis Greenacre
G.M.H.
Alan Richard Hale
Miss. L.M. Hancock
Mrs. Victoria E. Hankey
Winifred Harris
St. John Hartnell
David M. Hayes
The Rev'd Noel A. Hector
Mrs Minnie C. Hill
Lyn Hodgson
Edward J. Houghton
Rosemary and Jack House
Megan Hucker
Institute of Physics
Peggy N.K. Jefferies
Joan Johnson
Mrs. F. E. Jones
Mark W. Lawrence
Elizabeth Layton
Richard A. Lee
Dennis and Maggie Lewis
Mrs. M.E. Lillie
Dr. Douglas M.G. Lloyd
W.J. Lyes
Christopher Marsden-Smedley
John Marsh
Robert F. Moody
J.B. Morley Cooper
Alfred and Annette Morris
Dr. Timothy Mowl

B.N.S. Nicholson
Miss A.G. Organ
P.A. D'A Parkes
Mrs. N. Pearce
Donald Phillpotts
Miss K.E. Pickering
Gordon Priest
Elizabeth Ralph
Alison Ranken
George Graham Read
Hugh Roberts
Geoffrey A.K. Robinson
A.M. Rome, FRIBA, FSA
Maureen Sage
Agnes F. Sandbrook
David A. Scott, Dip. Arch
   (Leics), RIBA
Keith W. Scudamore -Ringing
   Master of The St. Mary
   Redcliffe Guild of Bellringers
D.E.S. Shellard JP
Janet Sheppard
Mr and Mrs Louis Sherwood
Professor and Mrs Peter Skrine
Graham and Felicity Smith
Robert A. Smith

The Society of Merchant Ven-
   turers of the City of Bristol
The Solen Press, UEA
Alec G. Stevens
Kenneth Stradling
Ray Stephen Surman
R. and J. Teague
Mrs. Vere K. Thompson
Michael J.Tozer
R.D. Vaughan
H.J. Vincent
Annette Watkin
Frank E. Weare
Eileen D. Webber
Colston West
Rev'd and Mrs M.A. What-
   mough
Sir George and Lady White
Emeritus Professor Glynne
   Wickham
Alan O. Wills
Robert Alvert Willis
Alastair M. Wood
Dr. and Mrs. Paul M. Wood
Keith Stuart Woodward
The Lord Wraxall